PLEASE, CAN WE KEEP THE DONKEY?

green press
INITIATIVE

Please, Can We Keep the Donkey?

A Collection of Animal Rescue Stories
by the Massachusetts School of Law Community

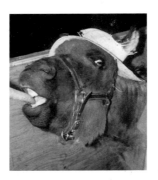

Edited by Diane Sullivan & Holly Vietzke
Foreword by Betty White

Lantern Books • New York
A Division of Booklight, Inc.

2008
LANTERN BOOKS
128 SECOND PLACE, BROOKLYN, NY 11231
www.lanternbooks.com

COVER CONCEPT BY MKV :: DESIGN BY WILLIAM JENS JENSEN
PRINTED IN THE UNITED STATES OF AMERICA

LIBRARY OF CONGRESS CATALOGING-IN-PUBLICATION DATA

Please, can we keep the donkey? : a collection of animal
rescue stories by the Massachusetts School of Law
community / edited by Diane Sullivan & Holly Vietzke ;
foreword by Betty White.
    p. cm.
  ISBN-13: 978-1-59056-122-5 (alk. paper)
  ISBN-10: 1-59056-122-8 (alk. paper)
  1. Animal rescue—Massachusetts—Anecdotes. 2. Animal
welfare—Massachusetts—Anecdotes. I. Sullivan, Diane,
1955– II. Vietzke, Holly, 1970– III. Massachusetts School of
Law at Andover.
  HV4765.M4P54 2008
  179'.309744—dc22

                                            2007047298

Contents

Acknowledgments

WE WOULD LIKE to thank the Massachusetts School of Law and Dean Lawrence R. Velvel for supporting this endeavor, the creation of the Shadow Fund, and all the animal law events held at the school. We would also like to thank Rosa Figueiredo and Briana Woods-Conklin for their assistance with this project, Kurt Olson for proofreading on a moment's notice, Rob Lynch for his creative help in coming up with clever titles, and George Bourque for his input and help with the Shadow Fund.

We also extend a very warm thank you to Kara Davis and Lantern Books for embracing this project and making it possible for all of you to read the wonderful stories that follow.

Our sincerest and most heartfelt thanks go to Laura Lussier, M. Kathryn Villare, and Michael L. Coyne. Their enormous contributions include, but are not the least bit limited to, sending the manuscript where it needed to be on time, making sure the stories were accompanied by photographs (and taking them if need be), working with Lantern Books, obtaining releases, and for oversight and assistance with all matters pertaining to this book. Without these three individuals, this book would not have been published, and we are most grateful for their help.

Finally, we thank you, the readers, for caring about animals. Your purchase of this book means that the Shadow Fund will continue to thrive.

This book is dedicated to Robert Burke and Shadow, his best friend and companion.

Introduction

THE AUTHORS OF the stories in this book had no idea they would see their names in print. In fact, the editors had no idea, either. The authors—mostly students at the Massachusetts School of Law—had a much more important goal in mind: receiving extra credit in their Contract Law class. It was only after grading all the submissions—some of which moved her to tears—that Professor Diane Sullivan thought these stories were too good to keep to herself.

We really have retired Marine Lieutenant Colonel Jay Kopelman to thank for this project. It all started when Diane arranged for him to visit the school to discuss his best selling book about a puppy he rescued in Iraq. Desirous of having him speak to a full room, Diane offered her Contract Law classes extra credit if they attended the discussion and wrote a paper about helping an animal. The responses she received were tremendous—both in quantity and content. She had no idea that a little school tucked away twenty-five miles north of Boston had so many students willing to sacrifice simplicity, family harmony, and even jobs to save or adopt an animal. It was then that Diane first got the idea to make a book, and we posted signs at the school, inviting other students and faculty to submit stories, too.

People have different perceptions of lawyers and the legal field, but "animal lovers" or "animal activists" is generally not one of them. What makes this book unique is the fact that here is a group of individuals, gathered in a single building to study law, that have a common willingness to help animals and various experiences of having done so. Animal stories are nothing new; we recognize that. But animal stories written by law students at a school with a total population of 600, who were determined to adopt or rescue an animal in need, are—at least we thought so. And as professors here, we are proud to be producing future lawyers with such compassion and concern for other beings.

As a side note, while this book was in production, we had a "rescue" experience of our own at the law school. One early morning in late May, our maintenance man Tim was greeted by a little Chihuahua-mix running out of the woods. Around his neck was a rope that at one end was frayed, as if he had broken loose from being tied up somewhere. With the nearest house at least a mile away, there was no way to tell where it had come from or how long it had been loose. As Tim tried to help the dog inside to feed it, it snarled and snapped. About an hour later, Tim and the associate dean, Michael Coyne, coaxed the dog inside with turkey Mike had in his office. That met with favor, and the dog's initial fear of Tim and Mike turned to trust. Once the dog was inside, it became immediately apparent that while it was out in the woods, it had been sprayed by a skunk. Mike wrapped the dog in an old sweatshirt to keep it warm, took a picture, and he and Diane posted "Found Dog" signs along the street, hoping to alert its owner, while Tim drove up and down an elderly complex nearby, looking for signs of the other half of the rope.

While we never did find the dog's original owner, we did find its new one. Diane remembered that one of our alumni rescues and adopts Chihuahuas. The only problem was that she lives in Connecticut. Nevertheless, Diane called her, and Dawn arranged to have her son pick the dog up that evening and drive it to Connecticut, where Dawn would foster the dog until its owner surfaced. If the owner never materialized, she said she would find the dog a home or provide one herself. Fortunately, the daughter of someone she knew wanted a dog, and this one turned out to be a great fit. It's good to know that the compassion continues even after the students have graduated.

Foreword

Betty White

Please, Can We Keep the Donkey? is a lovely collection of heartwarming occurrences to which all animal lovers can relate. Each story seems to trigger a personal memory of some animal that crossed your path—perhaps briefly—that you were able to help and that left a lasting impression.

How lucky we are that animals continue to serve as loving ambassadors in these troubled times. Let us never forget to appreciate them and make it a point to help whenever or wherever we possibly can.
You will enjoy this book.

Betty White
Actress and Author

1.

Please, Pick Me

Animal Adoption Stories

Stalking Hunter

John Burke

Hunter at adoption

IT WAS ON a late February evening in 2001 when we lost Mr. Pem, one of our favorite family members. We adopted him from a local shelter many years ago. He was the elder statesman of our canine clan. Sixteen years in a dog's life is about 112 in human years, but they were all good ones. He was a wonderful dog, and his loss was and continues to be very painful for us. Our other two family members, our Yellow Lab, Samantha, and our Norwegian Elkhound, Tigger, were lost without him. Mr. Pem was our Black Lab and as old as he was, he still managed to get everyone up in the morning to get them out in the fresh air, myself included. He was such a positive energy in the household. My wife and I decided that we were going to remember him and honor him by saving another dog's life and giving him a good home and friends to play with and keep him company. This is where Hunter's story begins.

Our decision was to find a dog that was truly not adoptable, a dog that no one would want. We started our search in late March 2001. We searched the Internet, the local pounds, and the Animal Rescue League. Unfortunately, we could not find that certain dog that we were looking to adopt. The dogs we considered were wonderful, and they would have made great family members, but all of them were very adoptable, and we wanted one that was not. We were looking for a truly unruly fellow. We were discouraged at this point. One of my sisters, who knew we were looking, called and suggested we visit the MSPCA in Brockton.

We arrived late on a Tuesday after work and began our journey through the nooks, crannies, and cages looking for our number three. There were many beautiful dogs and cats. Why would people give them up? The response I received from one of the staff members was "Landlords, divorces, children, and the worst: they just don't want them anymore." It was heartbreaking. At that moment, a woman brought in two beautiful grown boxers she was giving up because she was getting divorced.

As they were checking the dogs in for adoption, she was crying. She told the MSPCA staff member that the dogs needed to be together; they were not used to being apart. Their future was uncertain.

At that moment, as I was reflecting on the woman's predicament, I heard a crying and scratching at one of the adoption room doors. A little mixed breed dog was scratching at the glass door as he was attempting to leave a family of four. I was watching this poor little frightened puppy trying to make an exodus from what apparently was an undesirable location. The kids were trying to play with this terrified puppy, who obviously wanted no part of the mauling session. I approached one of the assistants near the adoption room where all of this activity was taking place and asked her what was wrong with the puppy, as he looked so terrified and lost. Then she told me the story behind his trouble and fear. He was part of a larger litter of puppies, who were beaten just for existing. He was the lucky one, the only survivor, but his survival was at a cost. He developed a terrible fear of people from the abuse. She then explained that there had been many people interested in adopting him; however, no one was able to reach him. I asked her what would happen to him if he were not adopted. "They have a timeline, and if an animal is determined not adoptable, it will be euthanized," she said. At that moment, I knew I found our guy. I asked her his name. It was Hunter. I told her I would be right back. I went over, grabbed my wife, and told her to come with me to meet someone.

We sat down in Adoption Room 2, where we were introduced to this multi-colored, scrawny, shaking little puppy. Cindy, the staff member who brought him over, was very nice; apparently, she had been the caretaker for Hunter over the last several weeks after his rescue and had developed a bond with him. Hunter's fear was evident. His body was shaking; his fur was at full attention, like a blowfish warning predators to stay away. I have had dogs my whole life, and it was obvious this guy suffered abuse. He was not receptive to us, as would be expected. Cindy left us alone, and we did not attempt to approach him. It became a staring and waiting contest. It was as if he knew the adoption rooms were available for a maximum of an hour and just watched the clock and waited. He seemed to know he would be done with us soon and put back to his sanctuary. Once we ended our visit, another staff member came in to take Hunter back; she asked us if we were interested in seeing another dog. She was dismissing Hunter altogether. My wife and I looked at each other and without saying a word to each other, we told her we wanted Hunter. The person in charge was directed to speak with us. He informed us the MSPCA will not let a pet be adopted unless it is a good match, and Hunter did not appear to be receptive to the two of us. Naturally, we started grilling this individual on the number of unsuccessful visits with Hunter already. We did not want this puppy to meet a bad end. He already had a terrible beginning. This person in charge immediately made another appointment for the next day. However, he made us understand that in the interim, if Hunter met a compatible family, he would allow the visit, and if Hunter was receptive to the family, they could adopt him. We had no options at this point but to show up the next day and hope he

was still there. We knew this puppy was not adoptable; he needed special care, and he was physically and emotionally battered. The only outcome for him at that facility was to be euthanized.

The next day, we arrived late afternoon at the MSPCA facility. As we walked around the facility, we did not see Hunter in any of the enclosures, and we became very concerned that someone may have adopted the little unwanted soldier. We asked the receptionist if she could set us up with an adoption room to have our second visit with Hunter. The receptionist looked through her records and said, "Hunter's gone." Dread immediately turned to fear, which turned to anger. Our first thought was that he was adopted, which was replaced immediately by our second thought, which was much worse. Instantly, the on-duty veterinarian was called over to discuss the situation of Hunter. "Situation?" I asked. She told us there was an incident last night with a family, and Hunter was removed to quarantine. I asked, "Why would you put a little frightened puppy into quarantine?" She said, "He bit a little kid last evening, and we have to keep him in quarantine for seventy-two hours." We explained to her that we were very interested in this puppy, and we came all the way to visit and possibly adopt him if we are allowed. She said, "We usually don't allow visits in quarantine, but it is obvious you care for this dog, so I will secure a room for you to visit him."

Hunter was already in the room when we entered, but this time was a little different, as if there were some divine intervention. He cautiously came over to my wife, while eyeballing me the whole time. He was not shaking or displaying his blowfish skills. He seemed a little more relaxed. Nevertheless, he did not approach me, which was quite understandable since it was a man who subjected him to such horrible abuse. This session went well, and we figured that if we got him home with our other dogs, he would settle in quite comfortably.

Hunter today

We met with the adoption counselor immediately after this session and said we wanted to add Hunter to our family. We said he would get along great with our other dogs. She told us that they would have to be part of the adoption process and would need to meet with Hunter prior to finalizing the adoption process. Although I was stunned initially, my understanding later was that other puppies were killed when brought to a home with full-grown dogs, so there was a need for this added precaution. We decided we would bring one dog at a time. Samantha was the surrogate mother of the canine family at our household and would be the best icebreaker, so we brought her first.

The next day, we brought Samantha into the main conference area, where the dogs are allowed to interact and make their own introductions. We remained in the room at all times, even though we knew Samantha's disposition was very maternal. Hunter responded to her quickly. There was no doubt: he immediately liked her. Off and on, Samantha would come to my side. As she did, Hunter would follow, wagging his tail, still cautiously eyeballing me, but showing a subtle form of acceptance. He probably felt that if Samantha was friendly with me, it might have been a signal that I was an "OK" man, and he should trust me also. You cannot blame him for being cautious. We were now down to the final test: Tigger, affectionately known as "The Big Tig."

We brought Tigger into the facility. Tigger is a Norwegian Elkhound; the breed is independent and somewhat aggressive towards other dogs, so we were very concerned about how he would take to another dog, especially a little puppy that he could easily kill. The meeting was like the first round of a boxing match; they were circling each other, and then it happened: Tigger's natural instincts took over, and he attacked Hunter. If he wanted to, he could have killed Hunter because none of us could have stopped him. However, the attack was more assertive, similar to an adult disciplining a child. Hunter then let Tigger chase him around the room numerous times, which tired Tigger out, and that was the end of the introduction. The olive branches were exchanged amongst canines. The staff that was there at the time was ecstatic; they wanted Hunter to find a home, especially Cindy.

Our adoption of Hunter opened our eyes to the cruelty to animals that goes on in the world and the changes needed to correct it. Animals are not commodities; they are creatures that feel as we do, and more people need to acknowledge that fact and respect them. We were successful in making a positive difference in one dog's world. Hunter is now six years of age and regularly runs around with Samantha and Tigger. That is one happy ending for him and us. But to this day, he still carefully eyeballs me at times.

A Tale of Two Shanes

David R. Mullaney

WHEN I WAS a young boy, I wanted a dog. My mom told me that I began asking for a dog when I was three or four years old. I won a puppy at a raffle at our church bazaar when I was six, but my mom wouldn't let me keep him. I remember crying in front of everybody there because I wanted the puppy so much. I think she may have felt she would have had to take care of him, and she was busy with my little brothers. Deep down, I think she wanted a dog too, but my dad wouldn't allow it. I continued to ask until my seventh birthday. It's funny how you remember certain moments from childhood; where you were, who was there, what happened. My seventh birthday was one of those times. My dad asked me why turning seven was so important. I had no clue. He said I had reached the age of reason, which meant I knew the difference between right and wrong. I remember the gist of my response: "Then tell me why it's wrong to have a dog." He said it wasn't wrong. I said, "If it's not wrong, then it's right, so let's get a dog." He didn't respond.

He also didn't let me get a dog. But the next year, I got the next best thing. Our neighbors got a cockapoo puppy named Shane. Shane ran into our yard the first day they got him. Mr. Buckley couldn't get him to come, so he asked me to catch him. From there it began. The Buckleys worked during the day, so they let me take Shane from their porch when I'd come home from school and bring him with me to play. I fed him, bathed him, and my mom even let him come in the house. On Saturday nights, he would sleep at my house with me. He was by my side from the minute I got home from school until I brought him home at night, which I hated to do. The Buckleys had a summer camp in the next town where they'd go on weekends, and Shane would stay with me. The summers were really great because he was with me from morning until night.

One night five years later, when I was thirteen, I was watching television with my brothers. It was winter. I heard a car screech its brakes, and then I heard Shane whimpering. I went running out into the street. Shane was lying in the snowy road on his side trying to move, but he couldn't. He was all bloody. The driver of the car that hit him took off and left Shane lying there. I picked him up, ran to Mr. Buckley's house, and screamed for him to open the door. We got in his car, with Shane on my lap. I kept asking Mr. Buckley if Shane was going to be all right. He didn't answer. I was hysterical. I didn't know where we were going. We went to the veterinarian. They had to put Shane to sleep. I didn't go to school for three days. All I did was cry.

I never bothered asking my parents again if we could get a dog. I waited until I had moved out on my own. As soon as I graduated from college, I went to the kennel, where I'd been many times to look at dogs. As soon as I walked into the yard in the back, I saw a cockapoo that looked like Shane. I bought him on the spot

The author, age 22 with Shane #2

for fifty-five dollars. The man handed me a receipt after I gave him the money. He asked me my name so he could put it on the receipt. I said, "Put the dog's name on the receipt; his name is Shane."

Shane was with me (and my subsequent family) for almost 14 years. He was there when my four children were born. My oldest son and my daughter remember him well. He slept with my son Ryan every night. It is difficult to describe in words what he meant to our family. He was brave and he was weak, he was fierce and he was timid. When voices would get loud, he would bark and calm us down. He was a peacemaker and a protector. He was a sight for sore eyes when I'd get home late at night from work. He was at my feet at five o'clock every morning when I'd have coffee before leaving.

Nine years ago, I had to have Shane euthanized. I had put off this day for longer than I should have, because Shane was suffering. It was a rainy Saturday. My children said goodbye to him, but at the time I don't really think they understood what was happening. I left the house with him on my lap in the car. I had the most awful feeling in my stomach. When I walked into the veterinarian's office, the staff saw the look on my face and brought us right in. They let me hold him as they put him to sleep. He died in my arms. It's killing me to write this. I walked out, got in my car, and didn't know where to go. I couldn't go home and face the kids because I was a mess. I thought about going to a bar and having some drinks to forget. But for some reason, I instead drove to church and walked into four o'clock Mass. I was embarrassed about how I looked because I'd been crying, so I sat in the back row. I didn't pay much attention to the priest or his sermon. However, I heard him say, "Be thankful for all God has given us."

Those words caused me to reflect on Shane, and how much he gave our family, how much of a positive impact he had on my impressionable children and my family, and how blessed we were to have him. He loved us as much as we loved him.

Bailey Winds up with a Wonderful Life

Laura Bryll

IT WAS AUGUST 2005. The phone rang in my kitchen. On the other line was my brother's friend Matt. Matt told us that his brother had a friend who had just acquired a ten-month-old yellow Lab from a foster home in New York City. The details were limited, but the friend needed somewhere to place the dog. Matt and his family were unable to take the dog, and he was wondering if we would be interested.

My brother and I were certain; a dog was just what we needed. We had one dog, and he would certainly love a friend. The only one that needed convincing was my dad.

When first approached, my dad said, "No, we do not need another dog." Matt called back and said that he needed to know in a couple days.

A couple days later, persuasion won my dad over, and we brought home Bailey. Bailey at the time was white in color and a sad sight. The dog was thin and certainly emaciated. When we talked with Matt's brother, he told us the tale of Bailey's last four months.

The man that bought Bailey was a businessperson who lived in New York City. Why he decided to get the dog in the first place is a mystery to this day. He left him in his 900-square-foot apartment all day. As any puppy is, Bailey was active and into everything. The businessperson was not happy with Bailey's curious nature, and he would often scold Bailey verbally and physically.

Not only was the businessperson abusive, but he was also neglectful. For the first few months of Bailey's life, he was not fed properly. When Bailey was hungry and in the little apartment for days at a time unattended, he would rip into the garbage for food. One day the businessperson returned to this mess and was extremely unhappy. From that day on, every time he would leave, he would lock Bailey in the closet until he returned. One of the neighbors in the apartment building called animal control and reported the treatment he knew to be going on.

Bailey

When Bailey was taken out of the home at only ten months old, the owner was more than happy to relinquish him. Bailey was tall and skinny. His puppy fur was leaving, and the fullness he had was disappearing to show his real physique.

On his first night at our home, it was apparent that he had been through a trying ordeal. He would not eat. All the coaxing in the world could not get him to even look at the food, let alone eat it. Bailey had been so badly abused that he was afraid to eat in front of our family for fear of the consequences. When he did eat, he gulped his food down so quickly he was sick after.

My aunt, who is a veterinarian and animal behavior specialist, checked Bailey out the next day. She put him on a special diet and explained that we needed to give him time and friendly praise when he eats.

It took weeks. Every time Bailey ate, we would pat him on the head and speak to him affectionately. In the first weeks, it was difficult because when we walked toward him and his food bowl, he would cower and stop eating. We would encourage him to eat by petting him and holding his bowl for him to signal that he was allowed—it was his food.

Eating was not the only obstacle to overcome with Bailey. He was also extremely skittish. In a home with a loud family, Bailey was constantly startled and hid when there was noise. He especially disliked the deep, loud voices of my father and brother.

My dad and brother were able to reduce the level of their voices, and Bailey soon changed his personality entirely. He was seeking out attention from our family.

He started to become more active and bubbly. Bailey was starting to get better.

His eating eventually became normal. You could pet him while he ate and even feed him treats from your hand. He gained weight, and he was extremely friendly. His tail was constantly wagging, a change from where it was between his legs when he first arrived. Bailey had become part of the family, and he loved it.

Now Bailey spends much of his day outside on our family farm. He loves to run and play. At night, he will snuggle up to us and lay his head on the pillow. He is a lovable, bright, and happy dog. I wish I could say the same for the cruel businessperson who mistreated him.

Please, Can We Keep the Donkey?

Lance Harrington

As a young child, I was forced to go on Sunday drives with my family to various places in New England. It was normally torture until one Sunday, when everything changed.

I was about nine years old at the time; my younger brother was five. We stopped off at a roadside general store in New Hampshire, which happened to have a petting zoo attached to it. Much to our delight, my brother and I were allowed to play with the animals; the owners seemed pretty laid back. We joyfully ran off with a handful of quarters for the machines that dispense animal feed and made our way inside the petting zoo. My little brother had taken off for the goats and sheep, but I took a different path. In the corner of the pen was a donkey, a Sicilian Donkey to be exact. I took a few handfuls of feed and approached him. He seemed a little timid, but once he found out I had a handful of food, we became fast friends. I couldn't believe how quickly he became personable and cuddly. We played with the animals for a little longer before going home.

Unfortunately, the family trips continued for some time. The good thing was, my brother and I were promised a stop at the petting zoo each trip. It was always the highlight of the trip. After about a year, give or take a few months, we stopped at the petting zoo one Sunday and saw a prominent going-out-of-business sign on the front door of the shop. At the petting zoo section, there was a sign indicating that the owner was willing to take reasonable offers for the purchase of the animals, provided they get a good home. As the Sunday rides continued, we would continue stopping at the petting zoo. Each time a couple more animals would be gone, having been sold. The "jungle" was thinning out in this petting zoo. The donkey remained, having no takers. It had gotten to the point where he was the only animal left. During liquidation of the store/petting zoo, the owners had draped a double-sided sign over the donkey's back with a price on it. At first it was $400, which got crossed out and re-priced at $250. This trend continued until the sign said "FREE." This meant trouble for my parents.

My family lived in Sterling, Massachusetts at the time, and my father had just built a fairly large barn that he was planning to restore a 1967 Chevy Corvette in. The barn had three floors and plenty of room for a Corvette. My brother and I decided that it would be much easier to keep a donkey in the barn as opposed to a Corvette, and besides, the donkey seemed more fun to us. After my begging, pleading, crying, and a temper tantrum of still unconfirmed proportions, my father uttered the now famous family words, "We'll take him."

The author with his new pet

The owner was extremely relieved. It turned out the donkey, Prince, had been rescued once before as an abused animal from a farm that an elderly couple could no longer care for properly. Once the owner confirmed our home was suitable for a donkey, he agreed to turn him over. Prince was immediately and properly re-named Chester Harrington.

Chester was a tremendous addition to our family. He was loving, personable, and despite the stereotype, incredibly intelligent. My brother and I quickly became pretty popular with the neighborhood children and adults alike. He instantly became a member of the family. I can still see my grandfather sitting in the backyard, lazily feeding Chester Lifesavers, with the donkey's head on his lap. Chester had plenty of room to run, and we could pretty much tie him up anywhere in the yard, seeing that we lived in a rural environment. On Christmas, we would decorate him in Christmas attire and tie him to a long rope on the front lawn. He never liked the hats and always tried to eat them. More than one family stopped to take pictures with him on our front lawn.

Our family had Chester for close to fourteen years before he passed away. His passing was a few years back, but every time I go into my hometown today and run across people from the old neighborhood, they always want to remind me of a funny story about Chester. The consensus favorite is the time he got loose from his rope and ran all the way down to the center of town, about a mile away, where he fell in love with the granite statue commemorating "Mary's Little Lamb," from the poem "Mary Had a Little Lamb," which is a true story that happened in Sterling. After a call from a neighbor who recognized Chester, I went to get him and walk him back home. Walking home that day, with my ass in tow on a short leash, and the people slowing their cars to laugh and take pictures of the situation, I realized three things: 1) donkeys run fast; 2) animals make people feel good and furthermore bring out the good in people; and 3) it was awesome growing up with the cutest ass in town!

The Tail of Olivia

Elaine Contant

The tail of Olivia, strong and multicolored, whips back and forth briskly at the sight of the peanut butter jar. With just the thought of possibly receiving a treat, the speed of the wagging tail increases, knocking over my favorite plant once again. But considering I couldn't even see Olivia's tail the first time we met, I'm always happy to see it now. The tail of Olivia, however, is just the beginning of the tale of her, not the end. The tail of Olivia is one of gratitude, graciousness, and glee.

There was instant gratitude between Olivia and me when we met. I first saw her at the Sterling Animal Shelter in Massachusetts. There she was, alone in this gigantic cage, curled up in a tight ball with her tail completely tucked under her. As I crawled into her cage and gathered up her warm, soft, fluffy body, I felt an instant sense of gratitude—gratitude for her coming into my life at that moment. Olivia, who felt something as well, slowly unwound herself in my arms, looked up at me, as if knowingly grateful that she was going to be adopted and brought to her forever home. That mutual gratitude has not faded one bit today.

Graciousness defines Olivia's being. She is the gift that keeps on giving. Every day she shows her generosity. It might be as simple as sitting quietly to allow a child to pet her. Or traveling two hours round trip to donate her blood through the MSPCA Blood Donor program. Likewise, Olivia's willingness to work, as a therapy dog providing companionship and comfort to those in need, brings pleasure to all those involved. Her actions remind me that true generosity, especially when offered from an animal, has hardly any borders. Olivia's generosity is measured in time, not money, in actions, not words.

Glee, as in *yippee*, describes Olivia's disposition. Such a temperament is great because even if one is having a tough day, she is right there as a breathing bundle of joy. Whether she simply places her head on a lap, licks a hand or nuzzles under the arm of someone dozing in a chair, she is saying, "Hello, I'm here, and I can make you smile." Likewise, every time she goes outside is like the first time for her. Her excitement is overwhelming as she bobs and weaves on the leash, not sure of which direction to sniff. Every time I come in the front door, she is so happy to see me, it's as if I've been gone for years instead of minutes. Pure joy.

Olivia

The decision to rescue a dog was simple. The likelihood the dog would be a mutt was high. My search for the dog began soon after my mother died in 2005. It is ironic that I've become a dog owner considering my father was not a fan of them. His lack of affection, I think, had mostly to do with the place where I grew up. We—two brothers, two sisters, mom and dad, and I—lived on the first floor of a two-family house in Springfield, Massachusetts. It was a tiny corner lot, but it had a nice lawn out front, and *all* the neighborhood dogs visited it daily. The children were expected to keep them out of our yard to prevent them from doing their "business." I've chosen to believe it wasn't the dogs (*per se*) my father didn't like; rather it was what the dogs left behind. Years later, I've decided my dad, who was a great man, and my mom (a cat person) would be proud of me for rescuing Olivia.

The trip to the Sterling Animal Shelter in Massachusetts would not have been done without the presence of The Fairy Dog Mother. The Fairy Dog Mother, known as "Margie," accompanied me to the shelter to make sure that any dog I chose was "Fairy-Dog-Mother-Worthy." Margie has owned dogs all of her life, including a Golden Retriever named Goldie, who lived seventeen years. Any dog lucky enough to be owned or chosen by Margie was guaranteed to have a happy and fulfilling life, including many, many treats. So her approval and blessing were essential.

It was at the Sterling Shelter where we learned that Olivia's mom, found abandoned and pregnant, was rescued by the Southside Society for the Prevention of Cruelty to Animals in Meherrin, Virginia. With great medical care and lots of TLC, she gave birth to three babies: a male and two females, one of them being Olivia. After a couple of months, Mom was adopted in Virginia, and Olivia and her siblings were brought to Massachusetts for adoption. By the time I adopted Olivia, she was the last baby left.

This tale of Olivia is not the end of her story but just the beginning of the hopeful things to come.

Guess Who's Coming to Dinner?

Kristen Howard

HIS NAME IS Spencer, after Spencer Tracy. He came to live with us as a companion for our Doberman Pinscher, Greer, when he was nine months old. He is also a Doberman, or that is what the shelter would have us believe, though to this day I will swear on a stack of bibles that he is a Rottweiler. Spencer was a rescue dog from the Doberman Rescue Unlimited of New Hampshire (DRU), rescued from a "kill" shelter southwest of Boston at the tender age of six months. Apparently, Spencer had been found running loose on the streets of Brockton, Massachusetts. Afraid of everything, he was found hiding behind a dumpster, which was apparently his source of food and shelter.

He had spent only a few months at the shelter when I saw his picture on the Internet. His ears were bigger than his head, his legs longer than his body. The only kind words to describe him were "awkward" and "sweet," and clearly he needed to be a part of our family. The rescue volunteer explained that he was very timid and afraid of "loud noises, sudden movement, affection, his food, his own shadow," and pretty much everything. She explained that we would have to spend a lot of time helping him adjust to living in a home with "kind" people because he had obviously been abused in the past. We were unequivocally up for the challenge.

According to the rescue volunteer, in depressed urban areas, it is very common to find dogs of a "fighting" breed wandering the streets because owners cannot care for them any longer. This is usually due to either financial reasons or incarceration (of the owner). In cases where the owner has entrusted the dog to a friend and that friend no longer wants to take care of the dog, a typical solution is to simply "open the door" and let the dog walk out. This is also common where the dog does not pan out to fit the temperament of the breed, meaning where a dog is expected to be fierce and isn't, the owner doesn't want the dog any longer, so he literally opens the door and lets the dog go. But where one door closes, another one opens.

Spencer

Spencer came home with us and found a new bed all of his own, a new play friend, and a yard to run in. We first understood how severe the abuse must have been when the screen door slammed on the front door, and he scurried for the smallest, darkest place that he could find. It took him two hours to come out despite bribery and gentle words of coaxing. Eventually he came out of hiding and joined the rest of his new family, peeking at us from around the corner. We knew he would join us in his own time.

Bedtime came, and we introduced him to his new bed: large, luxurious, and clearly overcompensating for his abusive past. He curled up and settled in, and we turned off the lights. Ten minutes later, we heard him whining. Our six-pound cat had evicted him from his bed. This was a sign of things to come. However, no matter how much effort we put into desensitizing him, loud sounds similar to gunshots would always send him scurrying for safety; some things are hard to forget.

Training him was a challenge and sometimes exhausting. We worked constantly with food protection issues, sudden movements, stepping over him, taking his toys, and preparing him for the poking and prodding that comes along with living with an infant. We would retrieve food from his mouth, put our hands in his food, tug on his ears, make loud noises, all to show that he could trust us to protect and care for him. We worked with private trainers who actually trained us, not Spencer, for we were the ones who needed training in how to care for an abused dog.

We had no idea what abuse he had suffered and could only guess at how long it would take him to relax and settle into what most would deem a life of luxury. Whatever that timeframe was to be, we were willingly in it for the long haul. This dog was sweet; there was not a mean or malevolent hair on his body. It was obvious to us that he was, and would always be, a scared puppy that had been turned out on to the streets to fend for himself.

I am certain he understood we were trying to help him and welcome him to our lives. Spencer learned to swim, boat, hike, camp, and laze the day away with his new family. Over an eight-year period, he did not even resemble the dog that we adopted. As we had hoped, he became part of our family, a companion to Greer, and we all became inseparable.

Don't Pet the Ugly Dog

Troy Daniels

"LAST ROW ON the left, against the wall, second cage from the end." He was the only dog not barking. I had a dog already and wasn't sure about adopting another, but I decided to go see him anyway. A co-worker had asked earlier in the day, "Did you know there is a Standard at the Centerville Animal Shelter?" I couldn't think about anything else for the rest of the day. The dog was emaciated to only forty pounds and was listed as black. He had been brought in a couple of days earlier with a Miniature Schnauzer; both had been "severely neglected and abused." The animal control officer said they had been left outside year-round and had very little socialization. The Schnauzer had already been adopted by a volunteer at the shelter.

When I saw him, he had been given a bath, and it was obvious that he was gray, not black. I talked to him through the noise of the other dogs and the chain-link fence that separated us. He sat quietly and offered his paw. I was hooked. I inquired about adopting him and was told that I would be fourth in line. I didn't leave the shelter with much hope. On Saturday I called to see how he was doing after his surgery (he had to be neutered) and learned that I could have him. I immediately drove to the shelter.

After it was established that he would get along with my existing dog, we loaded him into the car and drove home. He did pretty well on the ride home. But he was afraid of everything—the car, stairs, dog door, unfamiliar noises, furniture—even me. He had never been indoors and seemed more comfortable outside. He cowered every time we touched or talked to him. This went on for six months.

We've had Jake for three years now, and it is a little bit of a struggle to remember what he was like. He now weighs around seventy pounds. He has good muscle tone and exudes self-confidence. Jake enjoys his regular visits to the doggie daycare and a variety of parks. Madeleine, our other Standard Poodle, still teases him at the beach—but last summer it looked like he was quickly overcoming his fear of the water, too. He is socialized and well behaved at the park and in crowded places.

The author and Jake

He enjoys sleeping in a warm bed and loves playing in the snow; Standards are sometimes used in Iditarod races. Jake and Madeleine were initially indifferent toward one another. Now they are inseparable and never let each other out of their sight. Jake enjoys the extra hard Greenies™ and Milk Bone™ treats. He sits, shakes hands, howls at the chime on the clock, and does a "dance of joy" every time he goes for a ride (it is a combination of a jump, bark, and turning in circles all at the same time). He also bites Madeleine's feet to engage her in play.

The day I picked Jake up at the shelter, a mom and a little girl were in the lobby. The little girl wanted to pet Jake. Her mom stopped her and said, "That dog is ugly." He was pretty scraggly and very skinny. Now people sometimes comment on how beautiful a dog he is—he's the same dog; the only change is the care he receives. When I reveal that he was a rescue, the usual response is, "I've never seen a dog like that at the shelter." The shelter is full of dogs like that—they just need someone to care for them. Adding Jake to my life has been extremely rewarding and one of my finest life lessons. Sometimes I think I was lucky with Jake. I realize that it really wasn't luck—it was patience, praise, love, care, and a huge reward.

Sarah's Smile

Michael B. Leamy

About six years ago, I began my search for a Rottweiler puppy. I was traveling a lot and wanted a dog that would not only be my companion, but would also protect my wife. The Rottweiler breed is known for being loyal, protective, but not aggressive despite its reputation. Rottweilers also are known to be great companions and truly passionate dogs. My wife and I visited a breeder and were going to bring home a new puppy, but we really wanted to rescue a dog. So we made one last call to a local animal shelter. Bingo! It happened to have a six-year-old female Rottweiler. Upon visiting the shelter, we took this dog into the backyard; she was very quiet and nonsocial. Saddened by her response, we almost walked away, but then we learned that she had heartworm and would likely be destroyed if she were not taken, so we took her home.

At first Sarah remained very quiet, yet she always stayed at our side. Sarah would sleep at the end of our bed at night. The only time she was not right beside either my wife or me was when we were on different floors in the house. Sarah would then lay at the top of the stairs and face downstairs so she could keep an eye on both of us. As protective as Sarah was, she was even friendlier. I often joked that if my wife and I were sleeping and a burglar broke into the house, the only chance he had of getting hurt would have been if Sarah licked him to death. However, if that same burglar ever dared set foot in our room, well, that person would not have lived to see the outside of our house.

I often think about the first day I brought Sarah home. During the car ride home she took up the entire back seat, and I began to wonder what I had gotten myself into. My wife had only had cats, and now I was bringing home a dog that weighed almost as much as she did. Well, in the next six years, my wife and I learned that what we had gotten into was a great friendship with a great dog. Sarah was such a part of the family that it was more noticed when she was not around than when she was. One day when we were looking at buying a new house, we stopped at the site to see how things were coming. We left Sarah in the car and walked to the house and went upstairs. A few minutes later, we heard someone coming upstairs. We went to greet the builder but

Sarah, providing a comfortable resting spot for Colin

could not find him, so when we went back upstairs, Sarah was lying on the floor in the master bedroom, with a smile from ear to ear. This is the same place she would sleep for the next six years once we moved in.

One day while out on a walk, I was attacked by a loose dog. Sarah was on a leash and I did not notice the dog until he was on top of us. I let go of Sarah to get away, and in the matter of a single second, she had flipped the dog on his back and pinned him down. She did not do a thing to him until I reached for his collar and he snapped at me. Sarah then ensured I was safe and held him in place. I guess it was payback for saving her life—she had maybe saved mine or at least saved me from a lot of pain.

Sarah's personality and demeanor never changed. This was a dog that had been sick, and then abandoned at a shelter, and had been accidentally stepped on and knocked over many a time by my nieces and nephews. However, she remained the most patient and loving animal one could ever imagine. In those times when my nieces and nephews would run into Sarah, she would just give them a lick to make sure they were all right. My sister's Labrador Retriever is not particularly fond of other dogs. When Sarah went for a visit, he would growl at her, but Sarah would go over give him a big lick and off they would go for a day of fun.

Some people wonder how you can love an animal that doesn't understand how to love you back. My guess is that these people just don't understand unconditional love in the terms that my Sarah did.

Speaking of unconditional love, my wife and I recently had our first child. My son came home and was promptly greeted at the door by Sarah. From day one, she was amazing. Sarah was not known for being careful and delicate. However, with Colin she was. Sarah even seemed to lick him as softly as she possibly could. When Colin was crying or fussing, Sarah would come and get us and look in the direction of where Colin was, as if to say, "Hey he needs you. Let's go!" Well, Sarah just recently passed away after a long, happy life. My only regrets are that I didn't meet Sarah earlier and that Colin will not have her as a best friend to grow up with.

The Dog of Fertility

Rich Balano

PRIOR TO ADOPTING Baxter, we just wanted a dog. It seemed as though any dog would really do; after all, my wife Kim was turning thirty-eight, and we were childless. We'd been going through fertility treatments with disappointing results, and Kim's frustration needed a distraction.

Kim took the initiative and did some research on the Internet. She found several dog shelters that would soon have puppies for adoption. We ruled out a pet store for obvious reasons, not the least of which was the puppy-mill problem. After narrowing the list of shelters to a geographically proximate group of three, Kim switched from computer to the telephone.

The calls stopped at the first one after she talked to one of the animal handlers at the Sterling Animal Shelter in Sterling, Massachusetts and learned about the plight of the Sato. The handler explained to Kim that the shelter had just received a small "shipment" from Puerto Rico of puppies from abandoned dogs. It seems that every so often a group of volunteers heads down to the commonwealth island to rescue abandoned dogs and their puppies. We learned it is a very big problem in Puerto Rico. So big, in fact, that the dogs have a name in Puerto Rico: Sato.[1] They also have their own organization dedicated to saving them.[2] Stateside, there are programs like Sterling's, organized to collect donations and go rescue them.

In August 2002, we adopted a three-month-old Puerto Rican Sato Labrador Retriever mixed-breed puppy and named him Baxter. Baxter was identified as a "Lab mix," the label they give to all medium-size black dogs. If there is any Labrador Retriever in him, it isn't much. As an adult dog, he resembles more closely a

---

1 The name *Sato* is Puerto Rican slang for a street dog. It rhymes with *gato*, the Spanish word for cat.
2 See www.saveasato.org.

Border collie than retriever. Many people have asked what breed he is, thinking they too can acquire such a great dog. They seem disappointed when I tell them he is pure mutt and all the healthier for it.

Technically, we didn't physically rescue Baxter; someone else had already done the difficult work, but we could ensure that the rescue was final. Our job was to give him a good home and take him for plenty of exercise.

Apart from his favorite pastime of chasing squirrels and chipmunks in the backyard, Baxter has been to Montreal, Canada; he's been on boats; and he has been sprayed by a skunk. These are his more notable accomplishments. We have now had Baxter about five years, and he is happy and healthy. He has even brought us luck: He has two younger brothers of the human species

Baxter and the results of his good luck

who were born to us in the past three years, and they could not get along any better. His disposition is perfect for the big brother he is now. Baxter is patient with the two-year-old who loves to chase him with various toys. The two-year-old stops only when he wants Baxter to stop kissing him. In spite of the occasional annoyance, Baxter is highly protective of both and always helps us by letting us know when a diaper needs changing.

Our sons will grow up with Baxter. In approximately ten years, Baxter will teach them both an important lesson about life and the inevitability of death, but I don't dwell on that one; it can wait. In hindsight, I feel bad that I thought of Baxter as just a distraction—he is family.

Harley,
the Motorcycle Hater

John Hazen

THE TIME HAD come to find a pet companion for my then recently widowed grandfather, so my fiancée and I went straight to our local shelter. We had a family dog ourselves, and we have always rescued animals from the local shelter.

This time, as we toured the shelter and listened to the animal control officer describe the animals that were available and ready for a new home, there was one dog that followed me with her eyes everywhere I went. This dog was off in a corner all by itself in a red crate. Now, I could have taken home any of the dogs, but I was looking for a connection. Sometimes, when you look into an animal's eyes, you see something that's hard to describe, but it feels like you are looking into the eyes of another person. The animal sometimes even looks back in acknowledgment.

I realize you might be thinking I'm nuts, but if you have ever had a family pet that was so loved by the family that it became another member of the family, then you know what I mean. I could not find this connection in any of the dogs that the animal control officer showed us. I walked over to the dog in the red crate and started to talk to her. The officer interrupted and said that she was in no condition to be sent home with a family.

The animal control officer explained that the dog's prior owner was a deadbeat who had skipped town on his landlord. He had left the dog and her litter of puppies locked in a trashed, abandoned apartment. When the landlord came around looking for the rent, he found that the dog had been clawing at the door to the point it drew blood. All the puppies had died, and the mother was so starved that she nearly did not last the weekend.

The officer said, "If it gives you any indication as to what type of guy this deadbeat was, this dog's name was Harley." Apparently, Harley and her litter had been abandoned for close to a week before the landlord discovered them. The officer said that Harley needed to be spayed, given several sets of shots, and given more medical care than they were going to be able to provide. He said that the expense was not going to be worth the effort, because he feared that Harley was not going to be adoptable due to her extremely poor temperament. When left alone, Harley would bark non-stop until someone came into view. The real problem was,

The family Christmas card

I had the connection. I stood there, looking into this dog's eyes, not sure if I wanted to feel this connection with a dog that was scheduled to be put down.

I asked if I could take her out of the crate and see just how her temperament was. He replied that I could not

because she needed shots and other medical attention before she could be socialized. What happened next got me: Harley looked at the animal control officer, then back at me, and went to the back of her crate and curled up and lay down. I instantly replied that I would pay for the shots, spaying, and whatever else she needed. The officer replied that he had several animals in great shape, ready to go home that night. I replied, "If tonight's not Harley's night, then how many nights will she need before it is?" The officer smiled and said that if I paid up-front for the medical expenses, he would give her the shots and get her healthy enough for the spaying, but the temperament was up to me.

The deal was made, and I was writing checks and signing releases. I told my fiancée on the ride home that Harley would be my responsibility. I assured her that I would not be giving my grandfather a bad-tempered animal. I would be responsible for either transitioning

Harley into a family environment and or taking care of her myself.

As the days went by, I stopped by the shelter and checked up on Harley. She started to gain weight and look more healthy as they gave her the attention she needed. I brought dog treats and chew toys. It got to the point that if she saw me coming through the door, she would start running circles in her crate.

Finally, the day came when I was able to take her home. My fiancée came with me to pick her up. I had no problem getting Harley to come along with me. She hopped into the car and lay down in the back seat. We headed to the pet store to get her a bed of her own before going home.

She was a shy and timid dog when we brought her home. She definitely did not like being left in the house alone and would stand with her front paws on a window sill and bark non-stop until we came back into view. Other than that, she was the perfect family pet. We even found the perfect solution for the barking issue. We bought a twenty-five-by-fifty-foot chain-link dog kennel. We set this kennel up in the side yard and placed a dog house with dog toys inside. My grandfather and I played with Harley in the kennel for an hour or two each day. We did this for about a week before we left her in the kennel alone. When we finally did leave her in the kennel, she was fine. I don't know if she was fine because she was not trapped inside, or that she could see other people and/or traffic coming and going, but whatever it was, it worked.

Harley was a perfect house pet when someone was home, and when we needed to go out, Harley was excited to play in her kennel. Eventually, my grandfather started to just take Harley along to the post office and store. For a while during mild weather, my grandfather and Harley went everywhere together. When the weather got hotter, my grandfather didn't want to bring Harley along in the car and would just leave her in the kennel. After several months of bonding, my grandfather eventually started to leave Harley in the house when he would walk down the driveway and get the mail. At first Harley went nuts, but after a time of seeing my grandfather leave and come back, Harley would not bark like crazy but just yip at the window. By the time winter came around, my grandfather could even take the car to the bank and come back, and Harley would still be resting on the carpet by the coffee table.

Harley is now a regular member of the family. She has settled down and quieted in the past few years. My grandfather has even had a picture of Harley taken by the Christmas tree and used it as the family Christmas card. She can be left alone for easily a few hours with no sign of anxiety on her part. We don't press our luck because we don't want to upset her since we love her so much.

Sometimes, we even forget about her sensitivities, about what had happened to her. The only lingering indicator we have about Harley's past is that whenever a loud motorcycle goes by the house, she'll lift her head from her usual sleeping position and give a little growl.

The Art of the (Adoption) Deal

Christina Contardo

Mojo does not know she is a dog. At seventy pounds, she thinks she is a small person, and any "bigger" person's lap is fair game. Watching the Patriots game with a Weimaraner sprawled out on top of you, begging like a child for you to play with her, does not make for easy game-watching. "We have to get her a playmate," I said to my then-girlfriend Lisa.

I was insistent on adopting a dog; Lisa was insistent that Mojo like any potential dog we'd consider. Given Mojo's affection for other dogs, I didn't think this second criterion was going to be difficult to satisfy.

Visiting all the local shelters, I found several dogs that I liked instantly and wanted to consider. But Prima Mojo snubbed her nose at all of them. Not only would she not engage in any kind of playful exchange, she would not even sniff them. Sensing my frustration and wanting to head off the imminent plea for leniency regarding criterion number two, Lisa said, "Mojo *has* to like the dog—you know that." So I hopped back in the car for what would likely be another fruitless attempt at adopting a dog.

I arrived at the fourth shelter, not holding out much hope. I walked past rows and rows of empty cages—maybe fifty or more—and in the middle of them all was a single dog—a puppy named Levi—sitting with his head resting on his paws, looking up at me. There was not another dog in sight (I learned a few minutes later that the others were all out playing in the yard). I fell in love with him immediately, but then I'd already fallen in love with two previous dogs, only to have Mojo not share the love. I located a staff member and asked if I could take Levi for a walk. She tried to discourage me, saying it wasn't such a good idea. "He's in there by himself for a reason," she said, referring to the other dogs enjoying their play time. "Well, then, that seems like even more of a reason for me to take him for a walk," I countered. She still remained reluctant to let me. "He doesn't get along very well with people," she cautioned. "Well, maybe that's because no one takes him for a walk," I offered. "He has many issues that are far too difficult to deal with," she insisted. When I pressed her for examples, she said he wasn't housebroken. "So, because he's a puppy who isn't housebroken yet, I can't take him for a walk?" By now I was incredulous. Her answer: "Well, he won't be so cute when you have trouble training him." This went on for ten minutes. Finally, she granted me permission to walk Levi.

Trump

I took him outside and introduced him to Mojo, who, much to our surprise, was fond of him right away. She gave him the approval sniff and joyfully accompanied him on our walk, even initiating a play session. Levi was very happy to oblige, and while he was timid around us at first, he showed no signs of fear or aggression toward Mojo. After the walk, I told the staff member that I wanted him. "Well," she drawled, "he's cute, but cute is no reason to adopt a dog. There is a lot of responsibility here." Although I always appreciate being told I look younger than I am, at thirty-three, I didn't exactly think I looked like I was ten years old. As Lisa was putting the vein back in my neck, I asked what the "qualifications to care for a pet" were. Before she could answer my somewhat rhetorical question, I explained to the woman that I owned a house and a company, had a solid income and a lot of love to give, and that I was used to caring for a very needy Weimaraner. I assured her in a thousand ways that I am competent and patient and used to high maintenance beings.

I couldn't understand her reluctance to place him. This was a mixed-breed, seemingly "unadoptable" puppy in a no-kill shelter. I wasn't just "willing" to take him, I *wanted* to take him. And now I was having to prove that I *could* take him. After finally deciding that I might be Levi-worthy, the staff member gave me an application and asked me a series of questions, beginning with my job. When I explained that I was self-employed and worked at home, she asked what kind of job I had and what my hours were, as if I had lied about my employment. She then asked to see a copy of my lease, proving that I could have a dog. I told her again that I owned a house, and she asked who my co-signer (on the mortgage) was. When I said that I didn't have a co-signer because I owned it myself, she demanded to see a copy of my mortgage statement. Who brings a mortgage statement to adopt a dog? This was ridiculous.

She finally got around to calling my references, which I knew would not present any hindrances to the adoption. They wouldn't once she got hold of them, that is.

After receiving glowing recommendations from my first two references, the woman could not reach my sister, who was my third reference listed, because it was Sunday morning and she was at church. She thus would not let me take Levi, even though I explained exactly where she was and said that her recommendation would be just like the first two. By now I was beyond exasperated and said, "I don't understand why it is so difficult to give a dog in need a good home." The woman then explained that Levi had already been returned once by an adoptive family, and she wanted to prevent that from happening again. I asked why he was returned, and she said, "Because he was too much to handle." When I pressed her for details, she explained that a teenager and her mother had adopted him with the understanding that the teenager would care for him. After a week of Levi's shyness and accidents in the house, the teenager stopped caring for him, and the mother brought him back. I then told the woman that I wouldn't have spent three and a half hours at the shelter, pleading with her and answering her accusatory questions, if I didn't truly want Levi or would just return him. I also pointed out that it wasn't fair to the dog to let someone else ruin his chances of being adopted by a very loving and attentive family. "I assure you, there are no better people for him to be with," I said. "We treat our other dog like a daughter, and Levi will be her brother."

It didn't matter. She still wanted to speak with my sister, who I was now repeatedly dialing from my cell phone. When she finally answered, I put her on the speakerphone so the woman could hear her say, "I was at church—why are you calling me now?" I then handed the phone to the woman so she could hear for the fourth time that I was more than capable of giving Levi a good home.

Finally satisfied that I wasn't adopting a dog on a whim, the woman released Levi, whom I renamed Trump, into my custody. He was definitely very shy at first—and still is around new people—but he warmed up to me immediately. I think he was abused before, because he cowers whenever a foot gets close to him. He barks at everything that moves, and housebreaking was a very long process, but he has definitely settled down—and settled in, as there is not a pillow in the house without his signature teeth marks on it. And just as every child loves her pet, Mojo has a new best friend.

A Win-Win(nie) Situation

Diane M. Sullivan

My FOOT HITS the first step on the porch like a heavy anchor dropped deep into the black sea, another brutal day mercifully ending. While weary from the day's tasks, I know I still have dinner, laundry, and my reading. The key slowly turns the old lock in the door. A symphony filled with the sound of crashing containers and scattering feet makes me pause. I enter slowly. Winnie, shrieking with delight and boundless energy, flies through the air and gives me a kiss. No one before ever greeted me with such enthusiasm and passion. My day is infinitely better. I stand recharged. I cannot help but think... it was not always this way.

Winnie is a Chow born in a puppy mill. She was taken from her mother, put in a crate, and shipped north. She was then placed in a mall store window for sale at a handsome price. Looking like a little bear cub, she was bought on impulse, not careful analysis. Chows can be willful, protective, loyal, and like her Irish adoptive mother, independent to the degree of obstinacy. At first, things worked out well for Winnie, but then the economy turned. Winnie's family became homeless and began to live in a car because no one would rent to a family with three dogs and little money. Winnie's fur became matted, the car too crowded, and ultimately she was sent to live at an animal shelter.

As the days passed, Winnie became aggressive and hard to control. Winnie was in a kill shelter, and it was day fifty-eight. The clock was ticking. No one even came to look at her. Soon she would be one of the five million orphaned dogs and cats killed each year.

The shelter posted her adoptive information on the Internet. Her picture and hundreds of others were there for interested families, but Winnie's time was rapidly drawing to a close. I was haunted by her story. However,

I know my eight-year-old rescued Labrador Retriever Whitey is generally aggressive with other dogs. Maybe there was still some way we could make it work.

Whitey was not the only problem. My partner George didn't want another dog. He especially had no interest in an aggressive four-year-old Chow. He had even less interest in a Chow in rough shape that no one else wanted and that even the shelter said could not live with another dog. But Winnie deserved to be rescued, and I needed to help, having suffered my own share of losses over the last year.

A winning combination: Diane, with Winnie and Whitey

At the shelter, the animal behaviorist met me and asked a worker to get Winnie from her cage. Winnie was shaking and terrified. As I got down on the floor, Winnie came over and cautiously gave me a kiss. We bonded and then headed for home, finding comfort in each other.

My euphoria gave way to worry. Worried about Whitey's reaction. Worried about George's reaction. George was not home when we arrived. That was a relief. I could introduce the dogs without his watchful eyes. I put Whitey outside and brought Winnie to meet her new "brother." What a disaster! With two growling dogs both seeking supremacy, it could not have been worse. I decided to introduce the dogs by walking them together. I grabbed two leashes and away we went. Within minutes they were walking side by side getting along just fine; all happy, we turned to head for home.

Rounding the corner, I saw an unleashed Rottweiler come crashing through a closed screen door, bolt across the lawn, and barrel toward Whitey, Winnie, and me! He attacked. Whitey took the brunt of it. Winnie ran for her life, darting away through oncoming traffic. A van nearly ran her over, and then she was gone.

Screaming for help, I begged bystanders to find my dog while I attended to Whitey. A trembling and terrified Winnie was later found. I put her in the house to head to the veterinarian with Whitey. George then arrived home to a terrified dog that he did not want. Growling and snarling, a frightened Winnie would not let him in the house. This day just gets better and better.

George was so angry when I pulled into the driveway that I retreated to another part of the house and kept quiet. That silence was later broken when I overheard George say, "Okay, Winnie, you want to give me your paw…and a kiss, too. Good girl." Winnie certainly was appropriately named.

We all tend to live life on a schedule—with our own routines. Winnie broke our routine. Now every morning, Whitey, Winnie, and I get up with the sun, go for a walk in the woods, and conclude with playing ball in the yard. During Winnie's first walk in the woods, she was terrified. Crossing a little brook, I had to pick her up and carry her across. At every creek, snapping twig, or chirping bird, she stopped and trembled. Now, in the morning when I put on my hiking boots, she is so excited that she jumps high in the air with delight. She leads the way and runs over the creeks with abandon, chases the birds away, and makes her own joyous noise. Whitey, being a male, continues his habit of marking the trees along the way. Winnie has awkwardly learned to do the same. We all develop routines.

My routine is more or less the same. After our walk, I head out to my day's work of teaching at the Massachusetts School of Law. However, I am happier now and have hope that Winnie's story might encourage my students and others to pursue adopting one of the many dogs and cats that might not live without their intervention.

That Dog Rings a Bell

Michael L. Coyne

"**G**ET JERRY," JOSH said breathlessly. In a flash, his sister sprinted to the end of the cul-de-sac. She called out his name to find Hickory Hill's own Doctor Doolittle deep in the woods searching for snakes. Amy said, "Jerry, that robin's nest fell and hit the ground with the baby in it. What should we do?"

Neither Jerry nor Amy seemed to care that Jerry was only nine years old. With the confidence that only youth affords, they hustled out of the woods and up the street. Jerry always found more comfort interacting with animals of various shapes and sizes than with people. He would know what to do. If he did not, he would figure it out. If only all the world's problems were solved so efficiently.

They ran down the street to where the small crowd had gathered at the base of the large hickory tree. The snake he was holding made Amy's mother pause, but just for a moment. His eye first caught the cracked pale blue egg in the sturdy mud encrusted nest. He then noticed a very tiny bird with matted feathers and immature features with its eyes moving rapidly from side to side, as it searched for a familiar face but found none. Instead, the tiny bird saw a gap-toothed boy with the big round turquoise-colored glasses approach with his still-gloved hand. He entrusted the snake to Josh as he whispered, "He doesn't bite, but be careful."

As he gently picked up the nest and the startled bird, he knew that the mother, like his own, would soon start to search frantically for her missing offspring. "We need to return the nest as carefully as we can to the spot in the tree. I'll climb up there and someone can pass it to me," Jerry said. "I don't think so," Amy's mother said sternly, and they summoned Amy's dad to help. He brought a ladder and held it firmly against the tree as Jerry restored the nest to safety. Days later the robin was seen visiting the nest to feed her young, and the usual sense of order was restored to Hickory Hill.

It was that way over the years. Whether they started out as ours, like the iguana, snake, turtle, rabbit, and gerbil, or were found injured or orphaned like the occasional frog, turtle, or birds—many birds, for it seems sliding glass doors are catnip to our winged friends—they were nurtured at our house. As dawn follows night, animals would come and go, and Jerry would be there to take care of them. Nevertheless, he wanted a dog, and he wanted it more than he did any other thing in the world. In fact, one year he pleaded, "If you *please* get me a dog, I won't ask for anything for Christmas ever again." And even to this day, he is the only one of our three children that doesn't give us a Christmas list.

The problem with having a dog in our house was that his mom, brother Michael ("Mick"), and sister Kara all had allergies. Kara's asthma almost definitely precluded the notion of a wet, smelly, shedding dog running around the house. A few years before, we

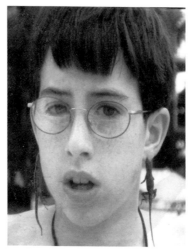

Jerry, the Hickory Hill Doctor Doolittle and . . .

gave up on having real Christmas trees. Each year Kara got sick from what we later discovered was naturally occurring mold that grows in the woods on evergreen trees.

For many years, we were able to forestall Jerry's desire to get a dog by telling him that he had a dog, but that it lived at his Nana's house. Then Nana got sick, and her little Shih Tzu, Precious, became a problem. In this case, while the breed's name appropriately fit this dog, its given name clearly did not. She was a biter. She bit everyone but Nana. As Nana's health declined, Precious continued to bring comfort to Nana and aggravation and anxiety to the rest of us. One day as Nana's health and hearing grew worse, Precious became trapped under Nana's motorized recliner dubbed the "Nana launcher." As the chair's motor ground slowly to bring it to a seated position, the tiny dog let out a series of yelps in recognition of the karma that had likely brought her to this place. In an act of supreme sacrifice, my brother rushed over to reverse the chair's movement and heroically rescued little Precious. In appreciation for his good deed, Precious gave him a nip. No, Precious would not be coming to our house.

To our surprise, a search on the Internet uncovered many dogs that shed little or not at all. They also appeared perfectly suited for life with the demands that young children can make. As our search continued, we grew more hopeful as Jerry grew a little less patient with each passing day. "I will feed him. I will walk him and train him. Please. Please. Please!" he begged. "Just give me a chance." Mick and Kara joined his fight when the doctor confirmed that some breeds do not present much of a risk for most allergy sufferers. Dogs are a lot of work, but we knew the joy that even one like Precious could bring to people.

Our search kept bringing us back to a Miniature Schnauzer. Schnauzers are highly intelligent, loving, playful, regal-looking dogs that were originally bred as farm dogs and rat catchers. Like its terrier cousins,

Sarge, the droopy-eared bell ringer

they are a good fit for allergy sufferers and are highly trainable. They are also generally tolerant of young children, even if at times they could be overly territorial and protective. An e-mail to a dog rescue worker was promptly met with a response. Indeed, she did have a little dog that was rescued from Kentucky. He had been bred for competition, but since one of his ears flopped down uncontrollably, his future as "Best in Show" was over. At seven months old, his fate was cast. He needed help, and Jerry needed a puppy. If it were true that one person's pain is another's good fortune, perhaps this would work for us all.

We piled in the Jeep for the two-hour drive to see the dog. There were still many questions to answer. Our long trip also meant the likelihood of carsickness. The barf bag had long been part of our family crest. Thankfully, with a car so full of excitement, no one had time to think about the ride. As we neared the kennel, I again made the obligatory speech saying,

"We are just coming to visit these people with the dog. He may not be a good fit for us. He may make us sick. He could bite like Precious. Let's take this slow, OK?" still knowing that a seven-, nine-, and twelve-year-old would translate that to mean: "We're getting a puppy today."

The approach to the farmhouse was off an old, winding, vine-lined road that stretched forever. We drove up the way and held our breath. Would this little dog love our kids as much as they already loved him?

As they jumped out of the car, the sound of barking dogs greeted us. We then made our way to the farmhouse door. Two kindly grandfathers motioned for us to enter. In the small, comfortable, classic New England sitting room, we made idle chatter and considered the suitability of this arranged marriage. It struck us as odd that the dog's name was Richard. Nana loved dogs, and growing up, we always had dogs and cats, but I could not recall any with a person's name.

Richard's long journey from Kentucky was made in ninety-mile increments. He passed from rescue worker to rescue worker while making his way north. He entered the room shaking and trembling. He could not even look directly at us. Richard was a small frail dog whose arduous journey and first few months left him scarred. When I got down on both knees, he slowly made his way over to me with head bowed. I held out my hand and then caressed him slowly. He quickly relaxed and rolled over on his back to show comfort and submission. I motioned to the kids to come near. He seemed soothed by their gentle loving touch. They bonded as one.

While they played together on the floor, I knew that there was no turning back. That little dog would be with us as our babies became teenagers and later went off to college. I hoped the fit would be as good as it looked. Still worried that his previous life might have left him ill-tempered and ill-suited to live with the cloying attention of three young children, we plunged ahead. "Let's take care of the paperwork," I said to the squeals of delight from three small kids, while knowing, as a lawyer, that love at first sight does not guarantee a life of uninterrupted bliss.

We carefully put Richard in the back of the Jeep with his blanket for the long journey home. He paced the back area at first but ultimately settled down despite the constant chatter and frequent stares from the children in the seat ahead. "Don't forget you promised to walk him early in the morning, and he needs to be fed twice a day," I said. "Oh, we will, we will," they screamed out. However, I knew those promises were as hollow as those made by the desperate souls who promise God in panic that it won't happen again if only he rescues them this one more time.

The lingering question of how little Richard would fit into our family was answered about forty-five minutes into the journey. The car filled with a putrid stench. "What is that?" I asked. "Not me," the voices rang out from the backseat. As they looked behind them, they saw what it was. "Oh, God, he puked," Mick said. My wife and I laughed. On every car ride over the last ten years, someone in the family got sick. On this ride it was simply the newest member of our family.

Little Richard became Sergeant Pepper for his salt and pepper coloring and Mick's love of music. He shed his timid demeanor and grew into the name Sarge. He patrols his house as the man in charge. He refuses to go to bed until Kara and Jerry come home at night, which for a college student like Jerry can be quite late at times. On the rare occasion when he somehow gets out without his leash, and we fear that he is lost or has run away, he immediately shows up at the front door with his head cocked slightly and this look on his face that says, "Where else would I go?"

One Christmas season, we put sleigh bells on the door to signal joy and good cheer to all who entered our home. Sarge quickly realized that by pushing the bells with his paw, he could signal us. Their ring now tells us it is time to take a walk or for him to eat. Those bells are now with us year round and throughout the year signal joy and good cheer.

Painted into a Corner

Lisa A. Gilman

I HAVE ALWAYS been a spiritually minded person, looking for the larger lesson in every experience. At one point a favorite author had urged that to give up all preferences was not only a powerful discipline, but should ultimately be the goal of each of us. I found the pondering of this concept thrilling in its radical stance, but quite frankly, there were plenty of preferences I was not interested in surrendering. These included a preference *not* to have golf, cheerleading, or toy dogs of any type in my life.

My eleven-year-old daughter's favorite movie of all time is *Legally Blonde*. Quite literally for years she had begged me to get her a Chihuahua. My vehement response time and again was, "That is the *one* dog that will *never* cross the threshold of my home." Well, the time came to consider a new addition to our family. We were well settled into a new home and for the first time had been without a pet. For months I quietly considered what to do, and when my daughter's birthday came along, I knew it was time to act.

I never valued an animal according to its pedigree or sale price, but to its nature. It wasn't that if an animal didn't fit in my family, it lacked value, but its value wasn't defined by pedigree or how much it cost. Since my daughter was still young at the time and had previously been badly bitten by a dog, I felt cautious of inheriting potential behavioral problems, and so I felt a puppy was a better fit for our family.

I started with the local SPCAs and found a dearth of puppies. I learned that New England was so progressive in its spaying and neutering campaigns and policies, that puppies were hard to come by. I did some further research and learned that SPCAs in the region reached out to other areas of the country to bring in puppies. I also learned for the first time of the Sato dogs from Puerto Rico. I finally settled on the idea of picking a puppy from a group arriving at the Danvers SPCA on the morning of my daughter's birthday.

On the morning of pick-up, I called to confirm that the puppies had arrived. They had not. This was my only plan for her birthday, so I was tempted to panic. But then I remembered a friend who had told me about a woman in Rye, New Hampshire who does rescue work. This woman is a technician for a veterinarian down the street from a pet store. When the pet store gets puppies from the puppy mills, many of them are half-dead from traveling in a truck with no climate control. This woman takes in the puppies that the vet feels he can't save and tries to nurse them back to health. I gave her a call.

The author, surprised at her fondness for a Chihuahua

When I arrived, there were only two puppies ready to go, and they were both Chihuahuas. In spite of myself, it was love at first sight. He was black with a white chest, white paws, and a white stripe down his nose. Here was one of the most perfectly ironic moments of my life. The perfect dog for our family was to be the very same which I had said would never cross the threshold of my home.

My red-haired daughter, then ten years old, had size eleven women's shoes, was the only girl on her basketball team and the new shotputting prodigy at her school. The puppy with the white markings, despite his diminutive size, seemed to possess the same irrepressible spirit my daughter does. I knew it was a match.

Later that day, I greeted my daughter in front of her school with Picasso poking out of the requisite handbag. He has been a one-man healing machine ever since. The blessings he has brought have been equally felt throughout our family, but one example illustrates it best.

Some may describe my husband as austere. He never smiles. An engineer by trade, he seems to always be looking for the imperfections in things. He is a huge man to boot. When I showed up with Picasso, he was horrified, embarrassed, and acted as if his manhood itself was under direct attack. Today he goes out of his way to show Picasso off, oblivious to the incongruous picture the two of them make together. Not only that, but Picasso makes him actually laugh—frequently, in fact—while Picasso commands all six feet five inches and three hundred pounds to chase him around the house; which begs the question: Who rescued whom?

Although I still despise cheerleading and golf, if giving up preferences nets these kind of returns, sign me up.

Happy's Trails

Caroline Hanania

It was the end of August 2005, when the United States witnessed another disaster. Hurricane Katrina swept into Louisiana. My family and I were glued to the television as we watched a whole state disappear under water; our hearts went to the victims who lost everything in a matter of hours. We wanted to help in some way. We saw these beautiful, selfless animals being lost in the flood without their families to comfort them. A friend of my mother told us that there was an organization that was trying to rescue the animals and find good homes for them. Unfortunately, if the animals did not find homes within a

Happy

certain amount of time, they were going to be gassed. All people would have to do was pay for the transportation of the animals. We decided to help by paying for the transportation to New York and any necessary medical treatment of a toy Maltese. At that time, "Happy" was only a year old; now he is three.

Of course, the organization was trying to find the original owners but couldn't. Happy arrived on August 28. He needed a few shots because of the potential for disease and infection brought on by the disaster. We chose his name because as soon as he was in a safe environment, you could see the energy and happiness in his face. Happy brought us such joy. He is the most affectionate dog that we have ever had. But not to strangers: In their presence, he is always trying to protect us. Nobody can step near the house unless we hold Happy first. We brought him from Louisiana to protect him, and now he is the one doing the protecting.

When my grandmother passed away last May, he felt our pain. He would not leave our side for one second. He had his little ears and tail down as he felt our great loss. I consider him my best friend. I found that the most interesting thing about animals is that their love and loyalty is unconditional. I was young when we had our former dog that died of cancer. I learned then that having a pet is such a privilege.

Happy has taught me courage and the value of friendship. Happy was one of the lucky animals that received a home full of love. Unfortunately, not all the Katrina animals were so lucky, and I only wish we could have saved them all. Happy managed to survive a disaster and still have a high spirit. All he wants to do is play, comfort us, and protect us. He taught me that although there are great obstacles in the world, one must have the courage and spirit to move on and learn from them. Now I look at obstacles as opportunities, not problems, and not excuses for me to give up.

Our Boy Scout

Sarah Fallon

WE HAVE ALWAYS had a family dog. When Josie, our fourteen-year-old Cairn Terrier, died of liver tumors, my family was absolutely heartbroken. We'd had her since she was a baby, and therefore she was an integral part of our lives and my childhood.

After a couple of weeks, my mother and I decided to adopt a new buddy. We visited local shelters and investigated ways to adopt via the Internet. After a couple of weeks, we found another Cairn Terrier hiding in the back of his cage at the Boston MSPCA. Scout was then five years old. He had been abandoned there only a few days before and didn't seem to be adjusting well at all. He hadn't been eating, was barely drinking, and refused to leave his cage and interact with the other dogs. We

Scout

got him to perk up a little, and then we knew we couldn't leave without him.

A few days later, we went back to the shelter to pick up our new little friend. As adoption papers were finalized, we learned Scout's story. For the first five years of his life, he had been abused and neglected. He had been brought in by the mother of the family who claimed to not have any time for him. He was a skinny little guy with a skin infection and some "unknown" breathing problem. After a couple of days at home and a course of antibiotics, Scout slowly began to turn around.

Scout, as charming as he is, is not without his idiosyncrasies. As a result of his past, Scout is absolutely terrified of newspapers. As soon as someone picks one up, he either runs into his cage or bolts into another room. Scout is also not exactly a quiet travel buddy. At first he may get all excited to go for a ride, but once the car is in gear, he has second thoughts and starts to cry. Scout will cry throughout the duration of the car ride, with the worst being the howling whenever the car slows down as if to stop. He is quite the nervous wreck when it comes to car rides and any time he fears being left behind.

Scout has now been in our family for two years. He is still very nervous and seems to get startled by the slightest of sounds. He quickly came around with his diet and is now quite the little hefty fellow. Scout immediately became part of our family, and it's horrible to think of what his life was before we found him.

The Love Pug

Laura A. Conte

I WILL NEVER FORGET the first time I laid eyes on him, all pink and soft. He could barely open his eyes to see his new world. I was amazed that in such a short time in this world—minutes—he inherently knew he was hungry and what to do to get his nourishment. Of course I had all the concerns most adoptive parents have: will he miss his mother, and will he cry for her at night? Will I be a good parent? On the day I was told he was mine and all the paperwork was finalized, I took him home and just held him for what felt like hours. Feeling his soft body, hearing him breathe, I knew then he was mine and part of our family forever. We named him Shamus, and he was a pug puppy.

I was nervous because I never had a dog before this. Most people actually tried to talk me out of it. They would tell me, "Oh, it is such a responsibility" and "Vacations—you can forget them now." I could not understand where the negativity about being a dog owner was coming from. Every time I saw people walking their dogs, they looked so happy. Yet I was receiving more advice against owning a dog than raising one. Why would it seem more stressful for our family? *I survived having two kids, I think I can handle a little pug,* I thought.

Then the first twenty-four hours occurred. In that time, Shamus had used my dining room, Oriental rug, my son's room, and my bed as his personal toilet. I did more cleaning and scrubbing the first twenty-four hours Shamus was home with us than I have done since I started law school in September.

I started to re-think my decision immediately and thought back on every piece of negative advice that I was given about bringing a puppy home with me. However, every time I was muttering some unkind words under my breath while cleaning yet again, I would just look at his scrunched up face that was usually right there with me, watching me clean, and I could not help but laugh. Every time I began to scold him for something he did, he would look at me, tilt his head to one side, and try to lick me!

I realized after the first couple of days with Shamus that owning a dog is not much different than having a baby. He woke up in the middle of the night crying, only to go back to sleep after I reassured him he was loved. My children, however, never ate my pillows or barked at anything that moved.

Shamus

After I adopted Shamus, it became immediately clear why so many people were telling me what a great responsibility having him would be. I realized that, in order for a family to own a dog, everyone must be up for the challenge. Of course, when our family was deciding to adopt Shamus, my thirteen-year-old son assured me he would "walk him every day." My four-year-old daughter, who was the most ecstatic that we were getting a puppy, vowed to "help out every day" with Shamus. (She was the one who named him as well.)

Well, at the sight of the first puppy accident, both my kids fled the scene. I am the one who does all the clean up, feeds him, and—for the most part—walks him. Only when my son has absolutely nothing to do does he offer to take Shamus for a walk. Otherwise, that task falls on me.

But even though my kids reneged on all of their so-called promises, I thoroughly enjoy taking care of Shamus myself. Part of me believes that it is some mid-life crisis I may be going through, missing the "infancy" of my kids. Nevertheless, I do love it. The solitude of walking him after a long day of work and a long night of school is therapy for me.

We recently had our first "illness" with Shamus. We had found a tumor on the top of his head, behind his ear. At first I thought it was only a tick bite. When the veterinarian told me that it could be something serious, I nearly fainted. After a short scare, we were told it was nothing, and he was going to be fine. As I look back at that incident, again I have to laugh at how frantic I was. He truly is a like a child to me. The emotional attachment to pets is unbelievable. Shamus instantly became part of our family, and we love him.

I am so glad we decided to make the leap and adopt Shamus. Although he is very precocious, I would not have it any other way! That makes him fit in all the more with us!

No Snowy Regret

JoAnn Riccio

AFTER MY LITTLE Yorkshire Terrier, Brandy, passed away from a collapsing trachea, which resulted in Primary Pulmonary Hypertension, I said I would never get another dog. Brandy had been sick for more than a year, and I had brought him to Angell Memorial four times in that span. His last two weeks, I slept with him on the floor at night to listen to his heart and breathing. I ordered oxygen for him and held a little mask over his mouth his last week to help him breathe. He passed away in my husband's and my arms. I told him it was okay to go to heaven, that I would see him some day, and that he shouldn't be scared.

So, after that, I just could not think of going through the pain of losing another animal again. That was until I saw Snowy's picture in the Sunday *Hartford Courant*. I saw these very sad eyes looking at me from the paper. The ad said Snowy had medical issues, and he was six years old.

I contacted Animal Friends of Connecticut, who told me he lived in a house in New Britain with sixty cats that were looking for homes, too. The woman who took care of the cats and Snowy was on medical disability, and she would get up every morning at four a.m. to wash the floors and feed the animals, and she would walk Snowy three times a day. He went to bed at 6 p.m.

When I walked in the house, I immediately smelled bleach. She told me she washed the floors with bleach every day to keep the house clean. There were cats everywhere: on the couch, on the sills, walking around my legs. I asked her where Snowy was. She said she kept him in a closed room. She walked me to the back of the house and opened the door. Way in the corner of the room in a pile of blankets, a little white dog was all curled up. There were several toys in the room and a bowl of water, but that was it. The woman told me it was best he was in the room by himself because of all the cats. He slowly got up from his pile of blankets and limped over to me. He was so little, all eleven pounds of him, and he gave me the lightest lick on my hand, and then he slowly turned around and limped back to his pile of blankets. I thought my heart was going to break.

The woman told me she had taken care of Snowy for almost a year, but no one wanted to adopt him because of his medical issues. I asked her what they were. She told me that his previous owner's boyfriend had thrown Snowy down a flight of stairs, broken his back, and he was never brought to the veterinarian to have it looked at. Because of that, he walked with a limp and could not even go up a stair. Also, he had thyroid problems and Cushing's Syndrome. She told me that if I did not adopt him, the shelter would put him down. She told

PET
OF THE
WEEK

SNOWY is a slightly handicapped, 6-year-old neutered male who has had all his shots. He is very lovable, but needs to be the only pet in a house without children. Inquiries for adoption should be made to Animal Friends of Connecticut at 860-

Snowy then . . .

me that several people had come to see him but left crying or were not interested due to his medical issues. I told the woman to give me a couple of days to talk to my husband. My husband asked me if I wanted to have another sick dog, and he told me that he would buy me a brand new puppy instead. I remember we were eating dinner at Chili's, and I told him no, that I wanted Snowy, and I wanted to take care of him.

My cousin is a vet in North Carolina, so I called him up and asked him to call the vet who had seen Snowy while he was in the shelter. My cousin told me that I would have to always pick Snowy up to go upstairs, and that medication for the thyroid and Cushing's could be costly over the years. I did not care. I called up Animal Friends and said I would adopt Snowy.

I remember going to get him. The woman bathed him and gave me his toys and a little woolen blanket. I paid $100 for him. I remember putting him in my car, and he seemed so scared.

This was a new life for him and me. I brought him into my house, and a few hours later, I put him by Brandy's doggy door so he could go to the bathroom. He just sat there. I figured with his injured back, it was too much to push him through, so I picked him up and carried him down the stairs to go to the bathroom. Later that day, my husband tried to push him through the doggy door, and Snowy bit him! I later found out from the woman who had him for a year that a man with a beard is the one who threw him down the stairs. Unfortunately, my husband has a beard and reminded Snowy of him.

That was almost eight years ago. Snowy is now going on fourteen. He does have multiple medical issues. I have four vets for him: His regular vet in Connecticut, a

. . . and now

respiratory vet and cardiology vet at Tufts, and a homeopathic vet in Vermont. They all know of each other and work together for his health. He now can go up four stairs all by himself, his coat is beautiful, and his eyes are still soulful. Sometimes I see the hurt still there, but most of the day he is a happy, energetic little dog that I love with my whole heart. I would never take back the thought of adopting him, and I know that from now on, I will always adopt a dog from shelter.

I have my own health issues that prevent me from adopting more than one animal at a time, but for now, Snowy is my main concern. I intend to make sure that every day he has left for the rest of his life, he knows he is loved and will never be abandoned again. That is my promise to him.

Ocy for Always

River Adams

MY DAUGHTER DOESN'T love our cat the way most children love their pets—as a toy, a playmate, a confidant for her short-lived secrets. He is all those things, but he is more. A symbol of her childhood. His name is Ocy, though it used to be Jake.

I stepped into the living room a few minutes ago to send her on some silly errand that had seemed so all-important, and found them sleeping on the sofa together, in such inviolable peace that it took my breath away, and all I could do was lower myself onto a carpeted step and hush, and stay, watching innocence like a movie.

She is spread about the sofa, leg on the back cushion, hand hanging off the side, long shiny brown hair covering the armrest and parts of her face. The furry symbol—not so much fat as generously proportioned—is resting on her chest, puffing up his belly in rhythmic breaths. They both have had a hard day. She played basketball, cleared the dishes, solved math problems, and zipped around the neighborhood on her absurdly long legs. He had two naps and a meal.

I am watching them sleep and wondering if she understands consciously what this cat means to her, and why she touches him with such care and gentleness, and why she reaches for him whenever tears are on their way. Does she know that he stands for her happiness, her security of being loved? Does she remember how it all started?

My daughter's name is Katie. It used to be Petra.

I found her seven years ago, in a standard way of the electronic age—on the Net. Her face in the picture was round, serious. Absent gaze. Circles under the eyes. She was looking into the camera with the resignation of a condemned soul taking in the barrels of the firing squad. A child prisoner. I searched her face for laugh lines and found none.

The file stated that she was in an orphanage. The orphanage was in Bulgaria. We packed our bags.

It's a long, painful process—getting a daughter. Waiting. Wading through the paperwork, the foreign language, the stupefying, maddening, hateful indifference of the people whose job is to love children. Plane tickets, passports, government officials. More waiting, the worst of all things.

We met her once and gave her back. We signed papers and went home to wait.

We met her again. This time they let us take her for a week. There were balloons, ice cream, and hotel television. New clothes. And, of course, a stuffed toy—a cat with black and white spots and ridiculously large ears. Then we went back home. To wait.

Almost a year later she was finally ours. We brought her across the ocean on a grand noisy airplane and showed her our house, her room and its walls, painted somewhat awkwardly with daisies and tulips—I had figured they'd be the easiest flowers to paint. Mixing

Ocy

our horrific Bulgarian with Russian with English with the most emphatic gestures we could muster, we explained to her that she was home now, that she was loved. That she was settled.

She smiled, clutched the mangled spotted cat, and eventually let me hug her. But in her eyes I saw the same steady resignation as in the online picture. She was only partly here. Just another place. And in her eyes I read the question: What this time? How long will this one last? How long before these strangers ship her back to the urine-stained mattresses, macaroni dinners, and a promise of life on the street?

Six months passed. Her English got better. I could now offer her my love in words she understood, and she accepted, gracefully, silently, submitting to the temporariness of the gift. I knew I needed help, and so I took my daughter by the hand, and we went to look for Ocy.

"What is this, Mommy?"

"This is SPCA," I said. "It's an orphanage for cats."

Her eyes darted out wide, and her hand tensed in mine.

"You can choose a kitten," I said, "and we will take him home with us, and he will be ours."

She kept looking at me and not moving, and I began wondering if she'd understood, when abruptly she turned and ran to the cages. Her eyes slid from cat to cat, hungrily, left and right, all over the room. Then she stopped, walked to a corner cage, and sat on the floor in front of it, sticking her fingers through the bars. She looked up at me, and the decision was made on her face.

She said, "Ocy."

The kitten in the cage was tiny, a few weeks old, covered in black and white spots. He swiveled his ridiculously large ears, toddled over to us, sniffed Katie's fingers, and yawned. This was the first time I heard my daughter laugh.

We played with Ocy and waited for someone to come out to settle the paperwork on his adoption. A few minutes later, she appeared—a woman in a lab coat. A veterinarian, as it turned out, she was bringing bad news: Ocy was sick, we couldn't take him. At least not yet.

What does he need? Medicine. Treatment.

How long? Maybe a week.

I turned to Katie, encouraged—it's alright, it's only a week! But her face was already red, and tears were swelling under the sticky eyelashes.

With a hurried goodbye to the doctor and a promise of another meeting, I picked up my wailing daughter and carried her out into the sun and air. On the curb in front of the SPCA, I let her cry it out, patiently, and only when her sobs turned into sniffles and she wiped her eyes, swollen into slits, did I take her hands in mine and speak to her.

"Remember," I said, "how me and Daddy found you, and came to see you the first time at the orphanage? We loved you so much, but we couldn't keep you right away. They made us give you back, and we had to wait. And it was very hard—so very hard, Katie—but we waited for you a long time, and then we got to come back and take you home with us. Ocy needs to stay at his orphanage for another week. But we love him, and we'll be back for him. He is ours now."

She was thinking, lips pursed, feelings passing over her face. Then she raised her eyes to me. They still carried a wet shine in the sunlight.

"Why is he ours?"

This was it. My moment. My chance.

I said, "Someone is yours if you love them, baby. I love you, and you are mine. My daughter. You love me, and I am yours. Your mom."

"So then...." She lingered, I held my breath. "So then, this is for always?"

My daughter was asking me if this was for always. I grabbed her in my arms and rocked her back and forth, and felt her moist little fingers squeeze the back of my neck.

"Yes, baby," I kept whispering into her ear, "it's for always. For always and always."

The Best Dog in the World

Stacey Healy

KIA, MY FIVE-YEAR-OLD Doberman-Rottweiler cross, is the best dog in the world. Although many may make the same claim of their dog, in this case, it is true. Kia helped me get over my fear of dogs. A neighbor's German Shepherd bit me when I was five, and I feared dogs from that day on. Kia taught me that there really are no bad dogs, just bad owners.

My husband Mark and I adopted Kia when she was nineteen weeks old. A family found Kia living outside and kept her for a few weeks. I believe they wished to keep her, but finances dictated otherwise. The family brought Kia to the shelter in New Hampshire, where my husband met her.

Kia's records indicated that she was used to living outside. The family had also kept her in a kennel outside. She did not have any signs of physical abuse, but the shelter staff indicated a concern of under-socialization.

Upon spending a few hours with Kia and reviewing her record, my husband decided to bring her home.

I had agreed to adopt a dog, but I was nervous. Learning that Kia was a Doberman-Rottweiler cross did not calm me. The first time I met Kia, my husband handed me the leash and left. I was truly out of my element. I had no idea what to do with a puppy. Kia decided to help me out by forcing me to action. She began to eat acorns. I did not know much about dogs, but I felt certain that acorns are not on any desirable canine diet list. I told Kia to drop them. To my surprise, she did. I then proceeded to open her mouth and remove the broken up pieces that did not drop out. After I removed my hand from Kia's mouth, I realized what I had done. Kia just stood there, wagging her tail. I took a deep breath, and we headed out for our first walk.

Over the next few months, Kia settled right in with our family. I learned about dogs through reading resources, watching educational programs, and observing Kia. Kia enjoyed learning tricks and entertaining people. Mark taught her hand signs to "sit," "stay," and "lie down"; she loved to show off. Kia quickly got used to sleeping indoors. She loved "bedtime," as she now had her own bed in our bedroom.

I frequently took Kia on walks in the neighborhood to socialize her, as the shelter recommended. Kia made a great number of friends, both human and canine. One woman in the neighborhood was an avid jogger. Each time we ran into her, we joined her pace for a block or so. The woman dubbed Kia her running partner; I did not get a title as I struggled to keep up with the two of them.

Mark and Kia took frequent trips to the dog park in Portsmouth, New Hampshire. I tended to watch from outside the park fence. Kia made friends quickly with dogs of all breeds and sizes. She eagerly picked up the game of "chase" and joined right in with the others. After a few trips, I became less nervous about the other

Kia

dogs and joined Mark and Kia in the park. Prior to getting to know Kia, I would not have even considered entering a park in close proximity to a single dog. In fact, I would have run at the sight of twenty dogs playing together.

Since adopting Kia, we have bought a new home with a fenced-in yard. We also brought a brother home for her, a Doberman Pinscher named Sumo. They both love peanut butter treats and running in the yard. It is a pleasure to arrive home to them daily. It is unimaginable that anyone would be able to mistreat or abandon animals that bring such companionship to people.

I find it amazing that I was ever afraid of dogs. Kia, undoubtedly the best dog in the world, showed me that dogs do not deserve fear and trepidation, but love and compassion. I'm not afraid of any dogs anymore. Now I fear only bad owners who abuse, neglect, or mistreat their animals.

For the Love of Cats

Mary Kilpatrick

MY NAME IS Mary and I am addicted to cats—specifically, I am a "softy" and currently have five rescued cats living at my house. Until last year and the death of my oldest cat Gracie, I had six. However, it is the cat that got away that often haunts me—the one I failed to rescue.

When I was born, my parents had two Dachshunds, but from the time I learned to talk, I begged for a kitty. Finally, when I was in third grade, my parents gave in. My mother had seen an ad in the local paper from the humane society featuring a beautiful, long-haired, tortoiseshell cat. She convinced my dad to let me adopt her. "The ad says she must be an only cat," my mom told my dad, "so we will have a reason to have only one cat, and she has already been spayed." This seemed to convince my dad, who was the last holdout.

So we drove to the humane society. The place was hot and miserable. There were lines of cages with frightened dogs and cats. This was long before current efforts in many parts of the country to make animal control and humane societies more hospitable and welcoming. I remember feeling depressed and overwhelmed. But a kind woman brought the tortoiseshell cat to me, and I held her in my arms. I was ecstatic; the cat was terrified.

We didn't have a pet carrier, so I held her in my arms in the back seat of our two-door Thunderbird on the way home. When we got home, my mother wanted to take the cat, but I insisted I would carry her into the house. As I tried to climb out of the back seat, she leaped from my arms and ran off. We searched everywhere for her in the neighborhood, and I sobbed for hours. For months, every time we left the house I would look for her, but I never saw her again.

In an effort to console me, my mother called our local veterinarian, who had rescued a cat who had a litter of orange kittens and arranged for my brother and me to pick out kittens. When we went to see the kittens, however, I fell in love with an older gray tabby and picked him instead, so we arrived home with Smokey and O.J. Then Snowflake, a neighborhood cat, moved in, and I brought home Kitten from school one day. (Yes, the cat's name was Kitten. I was going to call her Shamrock because I found her on St. Patrick's Day, but we all just kept

Two of the clan: Elsie & Oscar

referring to her as "the kitten." And since she looked very kittenish her whole life, it was appropriate.) After I left home, my parents rescued four more cats from the neighborhood—so much for my mother's promise to my dad of only one cat.

Prior to moving to Massachusetts, I lived in Florida, Maryland, and New York, and my current cats reflect my various stopping points. They include Oscar, a former feral kitten rescued from a dumpster; Oliver, a long-haired tabby with a humongous tail from a rescue group in Florida; Elsie, from a New York City rescue group; Simon, a former Bronx street cat; and Minnie,

a small white cat who came to us as a foster cat with small kittens and permanently established herself. Gracie, who was too private to ever tell us her true age, came to us rail thin with hopelessly tangled long gray fur and a heart condition. We had her for only a few months before she passed away. I brought her home from the Merrimack Valley Feline Rescue Society, where I used to volunteer caring for cats waiting for adoption, because her chances of finding another home were so slim.

I have loved all of these cats, but I often wonder what happened to the tortoiseshell cat who escaped from my arms, the cat I loved but never got to name or feel purr. I fear that she lived the rest of her life scared, hungry, and alone. My own rescue volunteer efforts and the many compassionate people I have met, who work to help homeless cats, have given me some hope she found a rescuer and perhaps received a second chance to find a nice family to live with, a family that would brush her long hair and let her sleep on the bed.

Fear-Aggression Strikes Out

Julie Williams

Tony arrived in New Hampshire from an over-crowded shelter in Radford, Virginia on April 6, 2003. He was found as a very young pup loose in the woods. Shelter workers assumed he was dumped there by someone who didn't want to care for him any longer. His new parents were waiting anxiously to meet him. Having been pre-approved for adoption, they were excited at the prospect of having a new puppy to make their family complete. The transporters had forewarned us at New England Doglift (a New Hampshire non-profit organization run strictly by volunteers for the purpose of re-homing dogs who have been surrendered, neglected, or abused through no fault of their own) that Tony, a twelve-week-old Labrador Retriever-mix pup, was not getting along with his companion Trey, an adult Lab-mix coming to New Hampshire from the same shelter. We assumed it was a result of the stress of the transport. We had no idea that this adorable little puppy would turn out to be the problem child that he was.

Tony was as adorable as we expected and was soon off to his new "forever" home. His new parents greeted their bundle of joy with great expectations, brand new toys, a new bed, and everything a puppy could want. They were simply ecstatic.

It was about four days later when I received a call from Tony's new parents: "Hi, we adopted Tony, and we cannot keep him any longer. He is out of control."

On my drive to pick up the little troublemaker, I couldn't help but wonder what this adorable little puppy could be doing to get him thrown out of his very first home, but I quickly found out. When I arrived to pick him up, I was shocked to see him running laps through the woman's house . . . up and onto the coffee table, over the kitchen chairs, even onto the kitchen table, as the adopter just watched him run wildly through. She then told me that he growled at them and bared his teeth (yes, this adorable twelve-week-old Lab-mix puppy) when they tried to get him into or out of his crate.

Tony's new mom quickly handed me his new crate, his new bed, his brand new toys, and his food and showed us the way out... almost as if she were afraid I would leave without him.

With all of our foster homes occupied and the possibility that this pup might bite someone, I decided he would need to stay at my house until I could figure out what to do with this pint-sized troublemaker. Soon I was off to Pet Agree to meet with our trainer, Karen Smith. I had no idea how to deal with these behaviors and needed to get some help quickly.

That was four years ago, and Tony is officially one of my "kids" now. I did attempt additional adoptions

Tony, practicing for "On Course for Kids," an agility fundraiser for children with cancer

for him, but neither lasted more than two weeks before we were called to go get him. He would behave for a day or two, and then he would revert to growling and snarling at people when he was afraid. Some say that Tony decided early on that he was going to stay with me, and others say I didn't try hard enough to find him a home. Whatever the case may be, Tony was a "fear-aggressive" puppy with the propensity to bite at a very young age. He was always on guard and desperately needed positive training.

Today Tony is my "trick" dog. He has his CGC (Canine Good Citizen) certification, and he is certified as a therapy dog with the Delta Society, a national organization that trains volunteers and their pets for visiting animal programs in hospitals, nursing homes, rehabilitation centers, schools, and other facilities.

He visits a local nursing home regularly and quickly brings smiles to the faces of the senior residents and staff. Tony happily greets children on his walk in the park and will eagerly perform his many tricks for anyone with a treat. This transformation in Tony did not happen overnight, but it did happen with patience, consistency, and positive training. Had Tony's behaviors been allowed to escalate, his future would have been grim. Tony is a true "poster child" for positive training and an example of what we can accomplish with a little love and concern for those more helpless than us.

Black Jack
Hit Me in the Heart

Stan Grayson

My uncle Dave was, for most of his life, a bird man. Considering Dave's chief interest in life, women, I often thought that a pair of love birds would be his ideal pets. But Dave wanted birds that could provide him with more interaction. He started with a parakeet or two and, as the years passed, acquired a Myna bird and then graduated to increasingly exotic parrots.

All of Uncle Dave's birds learned to mimic the affectionate vulgarity of which he was so fond. On rare occasions when my grandmother visited her son, Dave would proudly have the birds repeat what he had taught them. Perching on grandma's shoulder, they would merrily squawk in her ear things like "Love you baby," "Greeeaat boobs, aaaawwww!" or "Let's screw!" All this caused Grandma, as Victorian as one could imagine, to shake with uncomfortable giggles and she would return from her visits to tell, red-faced, how she had finally laughed until she cried.

Given the price of a parrot and the limited income Dave made as a door-to-door salesman of home improvements in Indianapolis, the purchase of his last bird, an African Grey, must have put a resounding dent in his budget. I never saw this parrot, but Dave always extolled its intelligence and speaking ability. Once, over the phone, he got the parrot to demonstrate, and faintly through the receiver came the undeniable cackle, "F__k me, baby, awwwwwhhh."

Except for family gatherings at my parents' home for Thanksgiving, I saw little of Uncle Dave. Our connection was maintained by occasional telephone calls, most of which, I regret to say, came on his precious nickels. From out of the blue, the phone would ring and there was Uncle Dave with his cheery greeting, "How are ya, kid? Getting any?" Then we'd catch up on the events in our lives. For Dave, this meant a reasonably graphic description of activities with his current lady and for me, a hopelessly bland update on career and family.

Black Jack

It was during one of these calls, probably around 1992, when Dave gave me quite a surprise. He reported that he had recently sold his parrot, a bird he always referred to as Darling although it was never quite clear whether this was an official name or not. "He got to be too much to care for," Dave said. "I got to thinking who would feed him if I had to go into the hospital. But I got a good price for him."

Dave must have sold that parrot when he was about seventy-five years old. Then he cancelled his subscription to *Bird Talk* magazine and lived without a bird or any other pet, but I could tell he missed his talkative pal. During our phone talks, he would ask detailed questions about the pair of Maine coon cats that lived with my wife and me. "Wonderful animals, cats," Dave would say. "So smart. And clean. I think about getting a cat myself sometimes."

The fact that Dave had mentioned the word "hospital" stuck with me. He had always worked out regularly and, as the years wore on, he remained in good shape, telling me how much he could bench press, how he'd won a grueling dance contest with a partner forty-five years his junior. Then, one day shortly after he turned eighty-two, Dave telephoned. "How are ya, kid?" he said. "I've got some news."

The news was that, a week earlier, doctors at the Veteran's Administration hospital in downtown Indianapolis had determined my uncle was suffering from esophageal cancer. The prognosis was at best guarded, which Dave translated as excellent. "They're talking to me about treatment options," he said. "It's a bad operation but they think the cancer is still very local so surgery makes sense."

My uncle had more news to report. Because he'd heard that people with pets live longer and have less stress, Dave had adopted a cat. "He's a marvelous animal, just wonderful. He's all black so I named him Black Jack. But mostly, it's just Jack."

Jack, it turned out, had been acquired for a fifty-dollar fee from Cat's Haven, a local no-kill shelter. Because the adoption arrangement involved the coop-eration of PetSmart, Jack arrived at Dave's little apart-ment in possession of a full complement of shots, feed-ing bowls, litter box, food, and a toy or two, all at little or no cost to my uncle. Not much was known about Jack's background other than the obvious fact that he'd been declawed. It was thought, however, that at some point, Jack had had "a rough time of it." But no details were provided.

To the surprise of everyone except himself, Uncle Dave came through the difficult surgery remarkably well. When I visited him a month or two later, he pro-nounced himself cancer-free, was going dancing once again, and was eating heartily. Jack had made himself at home by then. He seemed small for his supposed two years of age, but content. Jack divided his time between peering intently at the outside world through sliding glass doors that led to a small patio, or placidly stretching out in one favored spot or another. Once, I saw him asleep on the pillow in Dave's bed beneath the portrait of a fierce-looking tiger, a green-eyed reminder of my uncle's past glories. Sometimes, however, Jack simply disappeared amid the little apartment's clutter.

"That's why I put the collar with a bell on him," Dave said, gently stroking Jack who had curled up in his lap. "You can be looking right at this cat and not see him." This odd ability to blend, chameleon-like, into his background, was an ability Jack possessed either naturally or one that he had developed to an impressive degree. In particular, against a dark pillow or upholstery, especially in dim light, Jack, immobile as the Sphinx, became invisible.

For the next year or so, Jack and Dave lived happily together, and my uncle reported that it pleased him to have given the little black cat a home. "Every day I've had him," Dave said, "he's added comfort to my life. Plus, I'm feeling just fine!"

Subsequent to my uncle's illness, I began calling him more frequently, although it was clear he didn't really see the need for mere chat unless there was some-thing of importance to relate. That day came in the early spring of 2005. "The cancer is back, kid," Dave reported, "and they think it has spread."

This time, my uncle seemed to instinctively accept the news for what it was—a piece of bad luck. He'd lived a reasonably normal life for some eighteen months or more, but now it was time to make plans. I offered to come and help out with whatever needed to be done. In addition, I told my uncle that, if he had any misgivings about returning Jack to the Cat's Haven shelter, I would take him home with me.

"But you've got four cats already," Dave said.

"Well," I answered, "with that many, a fifth will hardly be noticed."

"That's real nice," he said. "Real nice. Let me think about it."

Having made the offer, a concern began to trouble me. It had less to do with introducing a fifth cat into the house than what would be involved in flying from Indianapolis to Boston with a frightened Jack. Whatever anxiety Jack might experience during the trip, my own promised to be far greater. So many things could happen, all of them bad.

The time for worry about the potential flight proved to be less than anyone anticipated. A few weeks later, I got a call from Dave's upstairs neighbor Ruth, a woman whose well-preserved figure he had long admired. Ruth told me that Dave had collapsed in his apartment, was talking nonsense, and it would be good if I could "fly out here quick."

"How's Jack doing?" I asked.

"Oh, the kitty," she answered. "He's must be there somewhere. Nobody can find him. He's probably scared, what with all the strangers coming in and out."

"He's there somewhere," I answered. "You can be looking right at him and not see him."

I arrived later that day, at about the same time as a hospice nurse whose assessment was grim. Dave was unable to speak properly but was alert enough to realize it, which was frustrating to him. As Ruth had said, Jack seemed to have disappeared. His bell was silent. We decided to have my uncle moved immediately to the hospital where it was eventually determined that hemorrhaging had caused his confusion. The next morning, after he'd received the needed blood, I walked into my uncle's room to find him sitting up and happily eating bacon and eggs.

"Hey, kid!" he said, buttering some toast. "When did you get here?"

The doctors didn't know how long Dave would remain in such relatively good condition. They could only guess a few weeks to a couple of months, but the transfusion had given Dave some much needed clarity, and he could assist in decision-making. Arrangements were made to move Dave to a nursing home, and I went back to his apartment and gathered up the clothes and other things he wanted. "I think you should take Jack," my uncle said that first evening in his new quarters. "I know he'll have a good life with you."

"Well," I answered. "We'll take good care of him. I brought a cat carrier with me just in case."

It was not until my second day in Indianapolis that Jack emerged to give me a few tentative sniffs. He seemed even smaller than I remembered, and I assumed that the comings and goings of strangers had been stressful. For the first time, I heard Jack meow. His voice seemed thin and surprisingly high-pitched, like a small cry. Then, with a brief tinkle of his collar's bell, Jack was gone again, lost somewhere behind the giant television and multiple VCRs that had provided my uncle with his primary entertainment.

"Well, kid," my uncle said when it was time for me to leave, "it's been great. And I don't want you to grieve too much. And I know Jack will be in good hands."

What do you say to someone you've known all your life but who will soon be gone? I had given this some thought and come up with no good answer. "Well, Dave," I said, "you've handled all this in a way that should be a model for us all. But I'm going to miss you no matter what you say. Don't worry about Jack, or anything else, though. I'll see that everything is taken care of."

"OK, kid," he said. I could see he was tired now, but a chemical patch was doing a good job of keeping pain away. "Let me know how Jack makes out."

"I'll call when we get home," I promised. I gave him a kiss and squeezed his once powerful hand. There seemed little that was left of Uncle Dave. He had become amazingly small. His once brawny arms were thin, the skin loose. I left him for a last visit to the apartment to fetch Jack.

Oddly enough, the cat came running the first time I called his name. There was the tinkle of the bell, and then Jack appeared like a puff of black smoke from the folds of a dark-colored blanket. As he'd had little or no recent experience with being placed in a pet carrier, Jack offered no resistance at all, and forty minutes later we were standing in line to go through security at the airport. I convinced the inspectors that Jack posed no danger and asked if I could take him out of the carrier in a quieter spot than the waiting line. Two of them accompanied us to a screened area and when I withdrew Jack, limp with fright, they quickly assured themselves that the carrier held no concealed explosives.

"We made it!" I told Dave on the phone that evening.

"How did Jack make the trip?"

"He did great. Once he realized there was nothing he could do, he just slept the whole way to Boston."

Getting acclimated to four other cats was a challenge for Jack. There were no hostilities, but Jack kept to himself in a spare bedroom, a space that we'd made available primarily for him. Within a day or two, however, the mutual curiosity that had developed among the cats resulted in a period of getting acquainted. Jack staked out a prime spot atop a sofa that gave him a good view of swaying trees, passersby, a few busy squirrels, and a varied bird population.

In just a couple of weeks, Jack went from sniffing curiously at the novelty of canned food to anticipation, showing up promptly at mealtimes and sitting patiently as the portions were doled out. Almost immediately, Jack's weight and size began increasing, and his coat seemed to thicken and soon turned as shiny as licorice. His sole problem involved becoming anxious or confused at unpredictable times. Sometimes, to the astonishment of the other cats, Jack sprayed when he should have gone to a litter box, and he looked hurt and sulked when he was admonished.

Uncle Dave was much relieved once he understood that Jack was settling in and comfortable. The news seemed to remove a last nagging worry from my uncle's mind, and I could sense the contentment that he felt. I reminded myself, however, that although Jack was here, in all the years since I'd lived in New England, we'd never managed to have Uncle Dave come visit. Now, it was too late. A few weeks later, at 3:30 in the morning, the expected phone call came. The nurse informed me that my uncle had died peacefully.

It took some time before I could fall asleep again that night. The windows were open and faintly, from the end of the street, I could hear the muted hiss of smooth beach stones murmuring against each other as waves washed over them and then receded. Otherwise, all was silent and the sky was peppered with bright stars. At some point, Jack jumped up on the bed. He appeared silently, for I had removed the collar and bell, and he hopped aboard so lightly that I didn't even notice. Then, after three pirouettes, Jack curled up on my chest, staring intently at me for a moment before closing his yellow eyes. How many times, I wondered, had Jack done just this with Dave?

So I thought then of my uncle and of his cat, my cat now, and the peculiar sequence of events that had brought Jack so far from the city of his rescue. Was it purely accident or mysterious fate that had guided Jack to my lost uncle and then to us? In the end, it made no difference. Jack was home.

2

Rescue Me

Stories about Saving Stray Animals

Puff-Puff, the Magic… Dachshund?

Geoff Healy

IT WAS A balmy evening in the summer of 1999. I was home on summer vacation from the University of Arizona, and on this particular evening, I was driving around the Methuen, Massachusetts area, along with two friends. We were looking for something to eat and had decided that the best course of action would be to seek repast at a Chinese restaurant in Salem, New Hampshire. The food there was palatable and competitively priced and became even more competitively priced as the hours of the night went on. Arriving at the restaurant via the sprawling back roads that connect Salem and Methuen, I parked my parents' red Caravan. Alighting from our beaten but reliable conveyance, my friends and I heard a clamor coming from the front of the restaurant. As the three of us approached the commotion, we noticed a car idling in front of the

restaurant, and beside the car stood a woman frantically calling for help. The three of us approached the woman and asked her what was wrong. Though she was not being particularly clear, my friends and I gathered something about a dog running around amidst the shrubbery that separated the front of the restaurant from the road. We assumed that the dog belonged to this woman. My friends and I fanned out, searching for signs of a dog. After about half a minute, I spotted a small, unkempt white poodle darting about the shrubs. I made a dash at the animal and grabbed her just before she reached the road.

I brought the poodle to the concerned woman, who had seated herself in the idling car. At this point she explained that it was not her dog. She had seen the dog running about and was worried that someone might accidentally run it over. Apparently the woman was with her son, who was inside the restaurant paying for a takeout order that they had come to pick up. Before we could come to an agreement about who would care for the stray, the woman's son came out of the restaurant.

This guy, to use the common vernacular, was a piece of work. He was sporting a sweater with a pastel pattern that even a blind man would recognize as being over the top and a mustache that would register about an 8.5 on the Chuck Norris Ridiculous Stache-o-meter. After the son had seated himself in the passenger's side of the car, the mother tried to explain what had happened regarding me, my two friends, and this scrawny, unkempt poodle. Upon hearing this, the son simply belted out a hasty "Just drive," which the mother obeyed. Thus I was left standing outside of a Chinese restaurant, slightly bewildered, holding a stray poodle.

Puff-Puff

After about a minute of dismayed staring, I realized that I needed to come up with a plan of some kind. I didn't want to set the dog loose, yet I didn't quite know what to do with her. Failing to come up with a solid plan on the spot, I put the dog in the van, and we went to get food and discuss the situation. After a greasy respite from the dilemma at hand, the three of us decided that I would keep the dog at my parent's house until I could notify the MSPCA in the morning. This was decided on the basis that my house was the most animal friendly. My family already had three dogs, so what would the addition of another dog for one day matter? When my friends and I came out of the restaurant, we found the dog sleeping soundly in the van. When I got home, I left the dog in the car and went into the house to speak to my mother, who is the more even-tempered of my parents. My father, thankfully, was asleep by this time. I told her what had happened and asked her if we could house the dog for the night, only until I could contact the MSPCA in the morning. She consented, and I brought the dog in.

The next morning my father woke up for work, discovered the new dog sleeping in the living room, and proceeded to wake up my younger brother and yell at him, believing my brother to be the one who had brought another dog into the house. My brother, not knowing what was going on, pleaded tired, tired ignorance. Eventually my father figured out that I was the guilty party and proceeded to wake me up and yell at me. The only defense that I could mount was that they, my mother and father, had raised me to be a caring and compassionate individual, and that simply abandoning a helpless, stray dog to the whims of fate was inconsistent with those teachings. This defense worked in the respect that my father stopped yelling. He was still very displeased, however.

The next day, my mother and I contacted the local MSPCA. From what information we gathered, we both concluded that, due to the disheveled and unhealthy state that the dog was in, the odds of it being adopted were slim, meaning euthanasia. Not wanting that, my mother began to contact local newspapers and police stations in an attempt to find out if anyone had reported this dog missing. It didn't appear that anyone had. No member of my family was surprised by this. The poodle looked as if she had run away or been abandoned and had been wandering around in the back woods of Salem and Methuen for some time. Much to my father's chagrin, my mother, my sister, my brother, and I decided that it would be best if we just kept the dog. It was a choice of handing the dog over to uncertainty (with one possible fate being euthanasia) or keeping the dog and ensuring that it would be well taken care of. My mother and my sister decided to name her Puff-Puff after a bit on *The Simpsons* television show. She was accepted well enough by the other dogs in the house and eventually came to believe that she is also a Dachshund.

This Bud's for Me

John Cutting

MY MASTER PLAN was set in action. It was a dream of mine to spend a year in Virginia Beach once I graduated from college. It was going to be the year of all years. I was going to spend the entire summer as a beach and water ski bum. Water skiing had come so naturally to me that I was asked to join the "Herb O'Brien" water ski team. This team was the largest manufacturer of ski equipment and the most sought-after team to join. It was a great honor to receive the invitation. I accepted and won many tournaments and actually became a very successful teacher once my knees could not handle the sport. All this took place before I was twenty-one. Many of my colleagues would spend the summer in Virginia Beach. So, the moment after I graduated, I packed my jeep up and prepared for the year of my dreams. I rented a cottage with my girlfriend Kerrie a half mile from the beach and a short driving distance to the local ski pond. After a long drive, we finally arrived at our cottage.

Kerrie and I unpacked the jeep and had our bathing suits on five minutes after arrival. Our next stop was to bring my boat to the pond where the dock was. This was a quick task since I was very familiar with putting my boat in and out of the water. Our next step was a drive-by of the cottage again to realize our dream had come true. As we passed it, we noticed a small puppy sitting on our porch. We figured it was the neighbors' and was simply confused as to which cottage was his, although we did think that the puppy was rather small to be out on his own. Nevertheless, we went to the beach and had a great day. I never once thought of the puppy that day: I was too excited about the summer. My mother always said that I was going to be a veterinarian. I have always had a love of animals and would get very upset whenever I saw any animal out on its own or being mistreated (the veterinarian thing did not pan out when I decided I would not be able to put animals down as part of my job, something I could not emotionally bear).

A few days went by, and I saw the puppy a couple of times during the day. I also noticed he was always alone and seemed to look dirtier and smaller as the days went on. At the time, I did not know that Virginia Beach was a common place for stray dogs and cats. I began to leave water and food out for the puppy. He would never take advantage of the gift. I remember looking out the window, hoping that he would drink and eat. He never did. Days went on, and the puppy was always around. What he was eating and drinking, I do not know. I was worried. I started thinking about this puppy at every moment. I would find myself wanting to be back at the cottage rather than behind my boat attempting some crazy trick for the camera. A few days later, my worst fears came true: the puppy was not around. I envisioned the puppy under some deck or in the marsh behind the cottage half alive or half starved, and I could not help. The torment that I went through was terrible. I could only imagine what had happened. Kerrie would always offer the bright side; she would try to tell me the puppy did have a home, and he was fine. This just did not work. Ever since I was a small boy, my mother always said I had this uncanny ability to feel the emotions of others. I'm not saying simply knowing when someone was upset. I would be able to feel the pain or know when someone was upset within three seconds of being around that person. I would also know when our family pets were sick or hurt before they even knew. I knew that there was something wrong.

Three agonizing days later, relief came. I was sitting on the porch when I heard a small, very faint cry. I leaped up and knew what the sound was. I quickly ran around the porch and there was the pup. He was in bad shape. He looked like he had not eaten or drunk anything for a long time. But he still would not come to me. How could I help this pup when he would run or scamper away when I tried to help? I called for Kerrie to follow the pup when I went to the local store to buy some dog treats. I must have purchased everything they had. I came back to the cottage with just about every treat. I even grabbed some cat treats in case nothing else worked. I returned and the pup was still there. What relief I felt!

Every attempt that I had made to get the pup failed. He finally came when both Kerrie and I would say to him at the same time, "Come here, Bud, you sweet little puppy love." He was starving and dehydrated. I probably should have taken him to the veterinarian or to the animal hospital so he could be in hands better than mine. (N.B.: He did go…just not right away.) The rest of the day, Kerrie and I spent watching Bud drink and eat to his heart's content. I was happy, Bud was happy, and Kerrie was happy. And he was going to stay with us that night in the cottage.

Bud

The next day—as luck should have it—the local veterinarian had an opening to see him that afternoon. While we were at the veterinarian, I had to explain how I got this puppy. I guess protocol says that the vet's office must take the pup to the shelter and do God knows what. I would not have this. It also helped that Kerrie started to cry. After Bud received a clean bill of health, we convinced the veterinarian to let us take him home.

We did attempt to find his true owner (if there was one). Kerrie and I put up "Found" signs. We walked Bud up and down the strip every day. We became his mom and dad. It could not have made us any happier.

For the rest of the summer, we did just about everything with Bud. He went in my boat while I would ski. We would walk on the beach. Bud even started sleeping in the bed with us. Bud became my best friend.

After the year in Virginia Beach, I landed a great job and was able to buy a condo that would allow me to keep Bud. I would not leave him because I knew he would never leave my side. He grew up to be a big dog. In fact, he grew up to be a very big dog. My local veterinarian said he must be a purebred German Shepherd. At two years of age, Bud weighed 140 pounds and looked like a small horse. He was simply huge. But to Kerrie and me, he was still the little puppy around the corner.

As years went on, Bud and I had many adventures together. Bud soon began to show his age. When I found Bud, I was twenty-one years old; I just turned thirty-four last week. I had to put Bud down last September. I will never forget the day I had to make that decision. Bud was sick, and I had to take him to the hospital; I thought he was going to pull through, but I was wrong. The veterinarian said he was incoherent, and his organs were starting to fail. I had to make a decision. It was difficult, but I made the right decision. When they wheeled Bud into the examination room, I was devastated. He was on a gurney (for dogs), and it was time. They said it would be painless and quick. I put my nose to his and said, "Hey Puppy Love." Bud wagged his tail as much as he could and twitched his nose. The veterinarian said that was the most Bud had moved in the last couple of hours. I will never forget Bud's puppy breath, and I will never forget his last breath.

Who Trapped Roo Rabbit?

Spencer Breunig

WHEN I WAS a teenager, both my brother and sister had rabbits. Hugs was my little brother's rabbit, while Fluffy was my sister's pride and joy. The problem with having pet rabbits is that they don't do anything. As much as I loved the idea of having a new pet in the house, rabbits don't fetch, they don't go on walks, and they don't like to go camping. They grew on me though, and I realized that although rabbits are not dogs, and not nearly as cool as dogs, rabbits love people and need affection in return.

A few years back I was hiking through the woods, and I noticed a spot where apparently some heartless individual had left one of those Have a Heart™ traps. I have no idea why someone would do something like that because those traps are meant to take animals like skunks out of urban and suburban areas, where they are both at risk and a nuisance, and safely release them into areas, like the woods, where they are neither. It seemed in this case that a baby rabbit had wandered into the trap and locked itself in. My heart was broken as I looked around, wondering who would do such a thing. The poor little fellow had eaten all of the grass that was available near the trap and was no doubt on the brink of starvation at this point, not to mention that there was no water available in the trap.

Not really thinking, I bent down and opened the door to let the little guy out. He immediately scurried out, in search of the aforementioned commodities. I decided that it would be best to remove this trap from its location in the woods. With the parking lot being not far behind me, I decided to bring it there and leave it where perhaps a ranger would most likely take it away. I then went back down the trail on my hike, no longer thinking of the baby rabbit I had saved only minutes before.

As I returned to the spot where I had first encountered the trap, I stopped short when I saw (what looked like) the same rabbit sitting in approximately the same spot I had seen him earlier, as if he was waiting for me. I walked up to the rabbit slowly, talking to it, and I put my hand out to pet it. The rabbit did not move as I approached, except to look up at me when I put my hand down. Still talking, I squatted down and started to gently pet the rabbit on the back and behind the ears. Was this a wild rabbit? Could it possibly have been a domesticated rabbit lost out here in the woods? There was no way the rabbit could have wandered this far away from civilization, could it? It was too small to have been any more than a few weeks old.

Roo Rabit

The thought crossed my mind that this rabbit might have been lost by its owners, and the owners set the trap up trying to catch it and that I had actually done a bad thing in setting it free. I decided that this could not have been the case because the setters of the trap would have put food and water in it before setting it and would have checked it at least once a day. This rabbit had been here longer than that. The thought then came to me that this might have been an abandoned rabbit. What kind of person could have done a thing like this? If someone wanted to abandon a rabbit, why not just let it go, or give it to someone who would love it?

The crazy thought then came to my mind that since my family had been without a pet for a few years now, they might enjoy the prospect of having a rabbit to take care of. This seemed like a ridiculous idea at the time, but I justified it with the knowledge that the rabbit would be free to leave at any time. So far, this rabbit had only been more than happy to see me and was not protesting my presence. I gently picked it up and cradled it in my arms. My parents' house is in a wooded area. This rabbit would be free to leave at any time, and I was pretty sure that we still had some rabbit food left over from when we had the two rabbits. We also still had the hutch. The hutch was safe, open, and comfortable, and I would let the rabbit out in the yard where it would be free to leave at any time if it so desired.

For some reason as I drove home, I decided that this rabbit should be named after a cartoon character. The only actual rabbit I could think of in all the cartoons I knew was Rabbit from *Winnie the Pooh*. Quickly, I decided that naming a rabbit "Rabbit" wouldn't be very original, so I thought some more. Tigger was my favorite character from *Winnie the Pooh*, but his name should be saved for a cat because he was a tiger. My next favorite character was Roo. Recognizing the unlikelihood that I would ever have a pet kangaroo, I made up my mind.

Roo is now my rabbit, and we are pals. He likes his rabbit food, but he likes a carrot and celery much better. He likes to run around, eat clover, and play. The funniest thing about him is that he builds things. It's like my rabbit is an engineer or an architect. If I give him two bowls, one with food, the other with water, he will finish the food and water and then stack the bowls like he is expecting someone to take them away and refill them. I take him in the house in the winter and give him boxes to play with. He stacks the boxes or arranges them in elaborate patterns that just blow my mind. He is three years old now, and everyone in my family loves him. When someone comes home from work or school, one of the first things he or she does is find Roo and say hello. In fact, I think I will go grab a carrot and some celery and say hi to Roo right now.

Seamus, the Cat Burglar

Dan Guerra

"Marion, we don't need another Goddard stray" echoed down the halls of the Goddard School of Science and Technology as my father realized he had just lost another stray animal battle. She had been at work since 9:15 a.m. on the rainy Saturday and found (or he found her) a tiny, flea-infested, soaking wet kitten. She had heard his cries and had opened the side door of the Goddard School, only to have him run through her legs and take refuge in her office. He had huge ears and a bushy tail like a fox, and his face was asymmetrically marked, making him look like a raccoon or Gizmo from the movie *Gremlins*.

He followed her into the kitchen area where she looked through the refrigerator for left-over food for him. This has happened countless times over the years, and countless times we all agreed that we would be keeping the lost soul that she'd brought home only until we found it a home. We always found them homes, and more than not, it was ours. My father is one of those men who has a bark but never a bite. He always says no and then brings the animal to the veterinarian for a check-up or shots or to be spayed. Once that happens, it has a name and a place on the couch. So goes the introduction of Seamus, the soggy, flea-ridden kitten who turned out to be my cat.

Seamus is a remarkable young cat. He looks Himalayan with long fur and markings similar to a Siamese cat. His eyes are sky blue, and he grew into his ears, which are now the appropriate size for his adult body. He established himself in record time at our home. In less than a day, we were all treating him like he'd been with us forever, and no one spoke of finding him a home.

The origin of these stray animals is worth noting. The Goddard School is a large inner-city school in one the worst neighborhoods in Worcester. The poverty is staggering. Ninety-eight percent of the seven hundred students qualify for free lunch. Yet in such a world, children still want pets, and parents still want to make their children happy. Many who take on the responsibility of a pet are unable to put food on their own table. Sooner rather than later, however, the family realizes that it cannot feed the animal or house it, and soon it becomes a ward of the street. We think this happened to Seamus. One woman told my mother that a family had moved out of the building, leaving kittens behind, which may have included Seamus. In any event, Seamus was the product of poverty and a society that turns its head away from many in need.

Seamus

As Seamus began his life as my cat, he quickly distinguished himself. He quickly learned how to ride in my jeep—a far cry from his first ride home inside my mother's sweatshirt, head buried so that he felt safe. He later learned to ride in my lap, paws on the dashboard, on small, local errands. In addition, he likes to study with me. He perches on the back of my chair and stretches out as if he is a head rest. No matter what time of night, or what the assignment is, Seamus is my constant companion and keeps me focused.

Everyone loves Seamus. We recently acquired two Golden Retriever puppies as a means to fill the void created by the loss of our Golden, Bridie. The puppies love him. They wash him, play with him, and work together to create havoc. If Seamus can reach it, then the puppies will reap the rewards. He will steal food, toys, and mail on the counters, and with great skill and joy, pass the sacred object down to the eager puppies waiting below the counter level. Last week, Seamus passed whole asparagus spears down to Gillie and Gallon until my mother caught him in the act. Between laughter and genuine frustration, she admitted to us all that she creates the insanity that fills our home.

Seamus is now eight months old and is one of the Guerra men. As he prances around wearing his bow tie and chirping out his version of cat comments on our every day occurrences, he brings joy to us all. He was a gift when I wasn't looking for one and a joy when I didn't think that I needed any more. He is an example of why strays should be adopted without hesitation. His first sprawl on my torts book said it all: "You're mine, I'm yours, and why that happened is a mystery, but it's a wonderful one."

Scene of a Rescue

Lee DiFilippo

Last fall, my wife and I were returning from a family event. It was late, a bit cold, and we just wanted to get home, see our daughter, and get to bed. Apparently, someone behind me wanted to get home quickly too, but this driver did not appreciate that I was following the speed limit.

The tailgater would not let up. Most of the ride consisted of high beams and swerving, which I saw in my rearview mirror. My wife became worried, as she believed that the driver was drunk. She commented that it was best to pull over and get the license plate when the car passed. I agreed as we stopped at a red light.

When the light turned green, I proceeded forward with the intention of pulling over to the side of the road. The driver pulled out to my left, hit the gas, and passed me with the speed of light. As she was pulling away from me, a cat ran out from the right side of the street, and the car ran it over. The driver never stopped, probably not even realizing that she hit something. The cat scrambled in frenzy and returned to the sidewalk, writhing in obvious pain.

I pulled over. I grew up in a home that included cats, and my family now has two cats (it was three until the third cat passed away a year ago). My brother and his fiancée have six cats. I just could not leave the cat as I saw it.

I moved in closer to see the damage. The cat appeared to be an older stray that was in extreme pain. As I approached, the cat hissed and was spinning in place, as it did not have the use of its hind legs. I could not see any apparent broken limbs, but it was obvious that the stray needed immediate help.

I told my wife to contact our veterinarian to see if he would be able to see the stray tonight. As she was calling, I grabbed my gym duffel bag and an old jacket I keep in my truck and returned to the cat.

At this point, the feline stopped scurrying around. The cat was breathing at a rapid pace but was still. It was not facing in my direction, which made it easy for me to throw the towel over the cat, pick it up, and place the cat in the duffel bag. I put the bag in the back of my truck and drove to the vet's office.

My wife was on the phone with the vet's answering service when it told her that the doctor would not come to the office for a stray. The service did refer us to Angell Memorial Veterinarian Hospital in Jamaica Plain. Jamaica Plain was a long way for me to drive, let alone be able to find that hospital. My wife then remembered an animal hospital in Woburn, where she once lived. We called the Woburn Animal Hospital for directions and told them that we would be bringing in a stray that was run over. The receptionist also referred us to Angell Memorial, as the MSPCA is located there and would be able to care and help get the cat adopted. I pleaded that there was no way I could quickly get to Angell Memorial, and Woburn was closer. Finally, the receptionist relented and agreed to take in the stray for examination.

I think that in most cases, people who rescue a stray would drop it off, thank the crew at the hospital for taking it in, and be on their way. I could not do it. My wife and I plopped down in chairs and waited. We tiredly laughed to each other because the person at the desk wanted to know what "our" cat's name was so she could fill out forms. I reminded her that it was not my cat, but that she could call him Pacino.

Later, the doctor appeared and stated that the stray was in bad shape. She gave it pain medication and would take X-rays to find any problems. The doctor then said, "By the way, *your* cat has fleas and is not neutered."

After the X-ray examination, the doctor said that she did not see anything obvious like broken bones, but there was a problem with the cat's hind end. She said that the hospital would keep the cat overnight and try to keep it comfortable. However, she did state that it would be best if the cat were to go to Angell Memorial. I thanked the staff for all their help and promised to call in the morning.

Sunday morning, I called the hospital to make arrangements to pick up the cat to bring him to Angell Memorial. I spoke to a nurse who was familiar with the cat; she told me that there was nerve damage to his hind end. In other words, the cat was paralyzed. A veterinarian who was also familiar with the situation then got on the phone. The doctor described to me what probably happened when the cat went under the car: the tail was run over as the cat was still running forward, also known as a "tail pull." The result is damage to the nerves from the tail to the hind end that control all movement in that area, including relieving itself.

The doctor said that I could take the cat to Angell Memorial, but even then, help and adoption would be unlikely. She recommended that the cat be put down. I paused when she recommended putting the cat down. I knew that this was not my animal, but now we had a history together. As I mentioned, I had a third cat, one that I took in from my parents because they were not in any condition themselves to take care of it. The third cat was one of the family cats that I grew up with when I lived at home. When he got sick, I had to authorize putting him down, which was absolutely crushing for me. Now, I had that same feeling for a stray that I had known for only a few hours.

I told the doctor that if she recommended putting him down, then that was the best thing to do. Another person was placed on the phone to witness my approval to put the stray down. I thanked the staff for the help; they went above and beyond. Never once did they mention anything regarding payment.

Although I feel bad about putting the cat down, we did as much as we could. If we were not there, the cat would have suffered, starved, and frozen to death on the sidewalk. He was cared for, medicated, and put down humanely. Unfortunately, that was probably the most care Pacino ever received in his whole life.

Casey at the Mat

Damaris Gayle

I HAD MY SHARE of dogs growing up. Because they have either died or been taken away for one reason or another, I decided that I would never have another pet. I began to associate them with emotional detriment. Until last year, I would not have even given a thought to having any kind of pets, not even fish. I would make all kinds of excuses for not having a pet of any kind. Then my daughter met Casey.

My daughter Sahsha is four years old and completely deaf. She has multiple disabilities, including developmental delays. Sahsha had only seen dogs and cats in books, and because of her developmental delays, whenever she saw a cat or dog on the street, she could not associate them with the animals in the book. She is the reason we have Casey.

Casey

I had just moved into my new apartment in the summer, and lo and behold we had mice—lots of them. My husband and older daughter kept insisting on getting a cat. Since I knew that I—not an animal lover—would be responsible for taking care of it, I refused. Then we started seeing a particular cat every day. Apparently, the tenants who lived there before us had abandoned her. The cat was always around the house. I was so annoyed by this stray cat that would always try and come into the apartment. Anytime the front door was open, she would run into the hallway. If we were bringing groceries in the house, she would run into the house and enter Sahsha's room. I wondered about the cat from time to time. I wondered if she was eating, where she slept, or if she was okay. But I just couldn't bring myself to have a cat. All I could think about was all the cat hair everywhere, smelly cat litter, shots, and vet bills. The last thing I needed was another mouth to feed and someone else to take care of.

Some time that fall, Sahsha and I were leaving the house, and Casey (as we started calling her) ran over to the porch. I didn't know if she was going to attack us since I would not take her in. Casey looked at Sahsha, and Sahsha looked at Casey, and then they both looked at me. It was the weirdest sight. All of a sudden, this cat and my daughter had some kind of connection. Sahsha just walked up to Casey and put her face in the cat's face. My heart just melted. It was the first time that I saw my baby acknowledge any kind of animal. I don't know if I was being a sucker for the cat or for Sahsha, but that same evening I went out and spent $100 for cat essentials and took her in. She has been with us ever since.

I now love Casey as much as Sahsha does. It is funny to watch them play. Sometimes Casey gets a little fustrated with Sahsha. In the beginning, I had to teach Sahsha that kicking the cat is not a good way to play, and she has slowly stopped doing that. Because of Sahsha's deafness, she doesn't have friends that she plays with outside of school. I think that is why she loves Casey. They don't have to talk to each other. The cat chases Sahsha, sleeps with her, and shares her toys with her. Watching them together just melts my heart. One year later, I still have to deal with the cat hair and changing the kitty litter, but honestly I don't mind one bit.

The Fed Baron

Anonymous

I THOUGHT I heard a noise that sounded like a dog yelping. Not seeing or hearing anything else, my brother and I kept walking. We were on our way to school, and, as usual, we had goofed off a little and were running late. We heard the sound again. Always looking for a reason to delay the start to our school day, we started looking for the source of the sound. When we found it, we couldn't believe what we saw. There in an alley, lying in a puddle of water, covered from head to tail with grease and mud, was a very small puppy.

On the outskirts of my neighborhood, there was a rundown industrial park that housed a dingy looking auto repair shop, an escort service, and an adult film studio. It was also used as a hangout for motorcycle gangs and drug users. Between two of the buildings was an alley that was at most eight feet wide. The alley was constantly littered with broken glass and debris. The dumpsters were always over full, and the trash from them spilled out into the alley.

During the day the puppy was kept chained outside in the alley. The chain was big enough to restrain a bull, which made it difficult for the puppy to move. Every day my brother and I would walk by on our way to school and would try to feed him through the fence. Most days we would be chased away by the shop owner or one of his friends, but every day we went back.

The dog appeared to be underfed and not well cared for, and he was always filthy. We never actually witnessed the dog being abused, but when the owner would chase us off, the dog would cower and try to hide behind the dumpster. You could tell that the dog was petrified of the shop owner. Through all of this, the dog never bared its teeth or growled at us when we would visit. When we sneaked him food, he would eat out of our hands like one would expect of a fully trained family pet.

One morning, when the dog was about nine months old, the police conducted a raid on the shop and upon finding drugs, several stolen motorcycles, and stolen parts, they arrested the owner and his associates. Animal control seized the dog.

By this time my parents knew of the dog and knew that my brother and I had been secretly visiting and feeding him. So the next day, my dad contacted the animal control officer and was told that although several people had come to see the dog, the officer had not released him because they could not produce proof that they could house him properly. My father met with the animal control officer, offered to be a foster family for him, paid the fees, and picked up the dog. The officer told us that the owner had violated parole and was already in the process of being sent back to prison. The

Baron

owner now faced new charges and would not be out any time soon to claim the dog.

After a couple of baths, several weeks of medication, and good feeding, the puppy started to fill out and was truly a beautiful dog. Since we did not know if he had a name, we named him Baron. Baron attempted to settle into family life, but unfortunately he had a lot of bad habits that needed to be worked out.

Because he was not properly house trained, we began crate training. He was very timid around strangers but soon learned to trust people. He suffered from separation anxiety and would bark if he was not in the same room with us. The most worrisome issue was that he was extremely aggressive towards other animals. With a lot of coaching and training, he learned to tolerate other dogs and animals. Given Baron's past, the separation issues stayed with him, so unless we went out, Baron had free reign to the entire house so that he could always be near whomever was home.

When we first took him to our veterinarian, the vet noticed that he had been tattooed with a serial number, which enabled us to track down the breeder. Through the breeder we learned of his show dog lineage and also learned how Baron had come into the hands of the original owner.

The puppy's owner had purchased him from a breeder of show animals. The dogs that did not meet "show standard" would be sold to families recommended to him by other breeders. When we spoke to the breeder at a later date, he told us that he would sell only to families, as he did not want his dogs mistreated or abused. He claimed that he did not breed dogs for fighting or to be used for protection.

According to the breeder, the original owner portrayed himself as having a family and so was able to purchase the puppy. Unfortunately this person had no interest in a family dog; he wanted a watch dog for his motorcycle shop and a fighting dog to entertain his friends.

Fully grown, Baron stood about thirty-four inches to the shoulder and weighed ninety-five pounds. He was an extreme example of what a healthy purebred Doberman Pinscher should look like. Because of the abuse he had suffered, we were concerned that he could still turn out to be mean-tempered, and given his size and strength, this was a big concern for us. Fortunately, Baron proved our concerns wrong and showed us that he truly was meant to be a family dog. He lived with us for thirteen years before he passed away from cancer. Wanting our daughters to continue enjoying the joys and love a rescued dog brings, my wife and I just adopted a Yellow Labrador Retriever from Indiana. Someone had stuck him into a mail drop box when he was only six weeks old. Fortunately for him and us, he was then given to a shelter that cared for him until he was well enough to be shipped here. Now he has three little girls who love him unconditionally, even when he chews their toys.

Italian Blessing

Gerald Delafano

ABOUT TWO YEARS ago, I met the woman of my dreams and decided to move in with her a year later. She and her daughter lived in a condominium complex in Plymouth, Massachusetts, where from time to time you see wild animals such as coyotes and wild turkeys running free all over the property. One day while taking the trash out to the dumpster, I noticed one of the smallest, most adorable little dogs I had ever seen, limping around the trash receptacle. At that point I was just hoping the little guy had not been hit by a car or attacked by one of the wild animals. As I approached him, I realized that the reason he was walking kind of strangely is that his nails were so long, he was actually walking on them instead of his paws. The poor little guy also looked and smelled like he had not

Roman

been given a bath in several months. He seemed to take a quick liking to me: he jumped into my car as I opened the door. At that point, I knew it was fate. He was very comfortable, helping himself to my lunch (peanut butter and jelly sandwich) sitting on the passenger seat. After he finished his snack, I decided to take him back to the condo, clean him up, and ask my girlfriend if we could keep him. Following a few minutes of bickering, she gave me the okay but insisted I put signs up around the city and check with the local authorities to see if anyone had reported a lost dog.

The next week I took him to get groomed and to the veterinarian's office for a check-up. The vet informed me that he was a male, mini-Italian grayhound, about three months old. About a month's time had passed, and still no one had claimed him. I checked with the local shelter, and then filed the proper paperwork to register "Roman" with the city of Plymouth.

Meanwhile, while all of this was going on, my grandfather of seventy-six years was losing a battle to colon cancer. The doctor stated the cancer had spread to other organs, and the situation was getting worse. My grandfather was in so much pain he decided to stop treatments altogether. My grandmother was devastated. We had just celebrated their fiftieth anniversary three months previously, and this would be the first time in fifty years that she would be alone, without her best friend. One month later my grandfather's time had come. This was extremely difficult for all of us, especially my grandmother.

I decided my grandmother could use a new best friend and companion in her life. The next day I arrived at her home and introduced her to the newest addition to her family. As I opened up Roman's crate, he nervously strolled out, looked at me, then looked at her, and I knew at that moment it was love. She was so excited to meet him, and for the first time in a month, she smiled. After I gave her instructions on his feeding and walking routines, she asked me if there was anything else she should know. I told her to make sure she stocked up on the peanut butter and jelly.

Dear Brutus

Neil Glazebrook

Brutus and I crossed paths ten and a half years ago at a time when we both needed someone to save us from the difficulties of life. At roughly four months old, he weighed only twenty pounds, very light for a male Pit Bull Terrier. I'll never forget the day I saw him hiding underneath the sofa from the cruelty the owner threatened him with. His small helpless body was curled up in a ball, hidden away in the sheltered darkness created by the sofa above, protecting him from the visual and mental torments that the light illuminated.

I had learned of him through a friend of a friend. At first I told him that I had no interest in having a dog; life was too busy and complicated. How could I take care of a dog? My attitude changed, however, when I found out that this dog was not being fed, and his health was dwindling due to the owner's lack of compassion toward it. My feeling was that the owner resented the animal for the burden he caused, though I never witnessed that. I told my friend that I would come to see him. The cramped, trashed apartment where I visited him was that of a man with a bitter face of resentment for all life. His distaste for the dog was apparent in the way he did not even call for him when I first entered the cave. The man only pointed to the sofa saying, "It stays over there, I never see it." There was no food or water for him and no record of veterinarian visits. I saw dead worms in the dog feces on the floor, which must have added to the hunger as the days wore on. He was a stray and was treated as such. His owner did not care to look for him—he did not even recognize that he was there.

"Forty bucks" was all he wanted, but I would have given anything to take him out of the darkness and give him what he deserved. All I wanted when I first saw him was to take him home and hold him. There was such an aching in my heart from this painful vision that I was compelled to save him. I quickly managed to take him to the safety of my home and give him a chance to live free from this mistreatment. His timidness and shyness took weeks to subside. But they did when he was ready. Watching Brutus's spirits transition into joy alleviated the difficulties that were playing out in my life. It was and is such a rewarding treat to come home from work and be greeted by

Brutus

his warmth. When I enter the house, his eagerness to come to my side to greet me with a lick eliminates any worries and complications that may have dampened my spirit.

I can't help but be envious of the way his life is so simple and innocent. He really doesn't have a care in the world now except making me happy and showering me with unconditional love. I'm so grateful for the way he always rushes to my side and leans his ninety-pound body against me. He sees himself as being smaller than he actually is, but it's welcomed all the same. He loves to be cuddled no matter where

we are. He always instinctively knows when to comfort me. He doesn't even have to make a sound: just being there helps. I still don't understand how anyone could have ever neglected him. He offers so much and asks for so little. When I look into those enormous brown eyes, I'm compelled to wonder what he thinks.

Everyone in my life is in love with Brutus. My parents are his grandparents. When they see him, they have treats for his visit; they babysit him when I'm away, and they allow him to sleep on the bed without any complaints. They fatten him up and cause him to always lose his manners. But that's okay because that's what grandparents are for. I blame myself for him thinking he's human, but I just can't say "no" to him. I just love having him sit by me and continuously arch his head back to let me know he's there (as if I didn't know by the constant weight on me). He is my best friend, and there's no companionship that I've ever felt that could even come close.

Top o' the Morning to Us

Diane M. Sullivan

I KNEW DAD WAS dying on St. Patrick's Day 2001. As sick as he was, he made us all the traditional Irish fare, but when he did not take one single bite himself I knew it was time to head to the hospital. I called his oncologist, and then we headed to the emergency room. Dad's blood count was so low from the chemotherapy, he was admitted to the hospital immediately. He never came home again, although he and I never gave up hope that he would. There were many ups and downs during his final nine-week battle with the cancer that ultimately claimed his life.

One evening, like so many others during Dad's hospitalization, I decided to spend the night with him because I knew the days were fleeting and he was suffering so. My partner, George, stayed with me until four a.m., but then he headed for home to get a few hours of sleep and feed his cat before returning to the hospital to sit with Dad while I went to work.

It was freezing cold that night in March when George headed for home. We were experiencing a severe cold spell, but I didn't mind because the weather seemed to match my mood. George needed gas, so he pulled into a self-serve Cumberland Farms and saw a dog standing near the trash, trembling in the cold. The dog then approached him, begging for food. Something was wrong: it was four a.m., freezing cold, and this short-haired, thin dog was looking for food at a service station. This dog's only identification was a tattered men's tie wrapped around his neck with a rabies tag on an unmarked collar. It was clear the dog had either been hit by a car or beaten because he had evidence of a blow to his head and a gash over his eye. George inquired inside. The attendant said the dog had been hanging around there a couple of days. He thought the dog had been living in the woods behind the store—for a short period of time, he lived among some "street people," who used the old tie as a leash.

A few hours later, when George called me to check on Dad, he told me he had found a dog. He said if he couldn't find the owner, and if the dog checked out okay at the veterinarian's, he would keep him. I remember thinking, *Even if the dog doesn't check out health-wise, you need to keep him*, but I also thought the dog's health was the least of his problems—my dog and his cat's reaction to this dog were bigger problems. George must have read my mind because his next question was whether I thought his cat and this dog could get along. I responded "Absolutely," knowing full well I was overstating the chances. I advised him to put up a divider and keep the dog and cat separated and just let them smell each other for a few days. So George installed a gate to keep the dog in the kitchen and away from the cat, but Christmas (the five-pound cat) decided to take matters into her own "paws": She promptly

The author and Whitey,
a little later than five a.m.

jumped the gate and jumped on the dog's back, digging her claws into him until he screamed. From that moment on, the dog never once bothered the cat, but I knew the bigger challenge would be my nine-year-old male Chow, Akuna. How would Akuna, the king, react to another male dog in his home?

We ultimately were able to track down the dog's owner through the rabies tag. He said the dog had been "a pain." His name was Churchill, and he had run away a number of times. He asked George if he wanted him. George said that he would love to have him once he had the dog checked by a veterinarian.

George renamed Churchill Whitey, after George's mother's family, the LeBlancs, which means "white" in French, or so I'm told. Whitey weighed in at sixty-eight pounds at the veterinarian's and received a clean bill of health. The only prescription necessary was some TLC and food. The big test, however, still was ahead: meeting Akuna.

When Whitey came to our family home, Akuna went on "full alert." A big scuffle ensued. We pulled these two alpha male dogs apart and put Whitey in a separate room with the gate. This time the gate worked; both dogs respected the boundary.

George looked at me and, seeing the horror on my face, simply said, "I guess we can't keep Whitey, huh?"

"Let's give it a little time," I responded, which was really the prayer of the hopeless. I was on overload. Dad was dying, my beloved Akuna was angry and upset, and this poor dog was scared and homeless. I think the two dogs could sense my despair and decided to call a truce—if not for themselves, then for me.

Dad died nine weeks later; Akuna and Whitey became best friends (well, almost), and we all moved to our current home in North Andover.

Whitey now weighs ninety-five pounds, and that's after his diet. Life is good for Whitey. Like most Labrador Retrievers, he gets up with the sun every morning, ready to go. (That was probably a problem with his original family.) He likes his breakfast early—and in fact has come to expect it—and then it is time for his hour or so run. When we return home, he goes back to bed for the morning. Unfortunately, I can't. So it is really good that I am an early-morning person. The first day he came to live with us, he thought three-thirty a.m. was a good time to get up. I have convinced him five a.m. will have to do. At the end of the day, Whitey has his supper and a final walk before he curls up for his night's sleep. He goes to bed early; after all, five a.m. comes quickly!

Last year, our dear friend and beloved Akuna died. After a painful period, we adopted a new companion for Whitey, a four-year-old shelter rescue named Winnie (see Winnie's story on page 50).

Take Mystic for Me

Joshua Burnett

I'M NOT WHAT you would call a "cat person." I grew up with dogs and have been around them my whole life. I am truly an animal lover at heart, but cats have always been a bit of a mystery to me. They seem to fit the aloof feline stereotype, whereas dogs seem more human than some humans I've known. I had never met a cat with whom I felt that human connection until I met Mystic.

During my junior year of undergraduate studies at UMass-Lowell, I moved into an apartment with some friends. It was a typical poor college student's flat. The only furniture was a couch, an easy chair, and a kitchen set, all of which had been handed down. In addition to the four human occupants were two cats and four ferrets. The last thing we needed was another cat.

There was at that time, and I'm sure there still is, no shortage of stray or neglected animals in Lowell. One in particular, a black short-haired cat, liked to hang around the neighborhood. He had iridescent yellow eyes and a peculiarly long tail. The last inch of his tail was bent like the knuckle of a finger.

It was one of my female housemates who first came up with the name Mystic. One summer day, my other housemate Michael came across a group of neighborhood kids (or should I say, punks) trying to sell a cat they had captured and confined in a box. It was hot, and I can only imagine how the poor cat must have felt trapped in a box. Feigning interest in purchasing the cat, Michael asked to see him. He peeked into the box, and peering back at him was a black face with yellow eyes. The kids never got their twenty bucks. In exchange for Mystic, Michael simply agreed not to beat them up. I probably would have threatened to call the police, but the threat of violence was more Michael's style. Regardless of how he was re-acquired, Mystic was safe in the care of loving humans.

We kept him separate from the other animals for a few days while we figured out what to do. He was surprisingly clean but a little mangy. But until we knew that he was free of disease and worms, we didn't dare risk exposure to the other cats. At first, the consensus was to bring him to the SPCA shelter near the south campus of the school. Six animals was enough. Besides, we had no idea how he would react to the others, especially the poor ferrets who might look to him more like food than roommates. We checked with the shelter and the police to see if anyone had reported a missing cat fitting Mystic's description. It seemed obvious that the answer would be "no," since we had seen him around for months, but we wanted to know for certain that he wasn't missed by anyone. Once it was obvious that he was abandoned, it was an easy decision to keep him.

I related the story to a professor, who offered to help with the veterinary bills. We were relieved to learn that he was healthy, and so he was released from quarantine and joined the rest of the household. There were a few scuffles as is to be expected with three male cats, but after the initial posturing, things calmed down, and to everyone's relief, Mystic had no interest in the ferrets. But he did take particular interest in me.

It started with licking—kind of a strange thing for a cat. Any time I sat down to watch television, he would jump up on my lap, lie down on my chest, and drag his sandpaper tongue along my neck and chin. If I picked him up and put him on the floor, he was back on me before I could resituate myself. I learned, or should I say, he trained me, pretty quickly to let him lick until he was satisfied, which usually took around fifteen minutes. He never did it to anyone else.

Then he started to follow me around the house with an infuriating yet endearing curiosity not unlike my fifteen-month-old son now does. I couldn't pour a bowl of cereal or open a bottle without first letting him investigate it as if he were my personal food tester. As with the licking, I was the only one who received this attention.

Whatever the reason, Mystic bonded with me more than he did with my roommates. Perhaps he sensed my love of animals, but the others shared that same love. Or perhaps he knew that I was somewhat ambivalent toward cats and took it as a challenge to change my attitude. Whether it was the last reason or not, that's what he did. I gradually became as attached to him as I did to any pet I had ever had.

After college ended, I was unable to take him with me. I was returning to my parents' house, which was home to two rambunctious Schipperkes. But I wasn't willing to leave Mystic behind with just anyone or anywhere. Fortunately, my roommate's mother agreed to take him, so he moved to Middleton, where he was loved and well cared for. I miss Mystic, but I will always have him to thank for showing me the human side of cats.

Snow's Plight

Dorian Furr

SEVERAL MONTHS AGO, there had been a stray cat walking around my house for weeks. As the weeks went on, I continued to see the cat. Eventually I began to put food and water out for it to eat and drink in my front yard. I live on a main street in Boston, Massachusetts, and many cars drive up and down my street. The excessive speed of the cars has caused the deaths of many animals on my street. One day, I noticed the cat was bleeding, possibly from an injury caused by one of the speeding cars. Because I now felt responsible for this poor kitten, I brought her inside and called veterinarians in the area to get help for her. Angell Memorial Animal Hospital agreed to look at her.

Snow

The kitten had many severe breaks in her little bones. But I was not going to put her down! I could not afford the vet bills that I knew would be in the thousands. I then searched for help. I come from a very large family—I have twenty sisters and brothers, and many more aunts and uncles—and I called everyone. My mother, sisters, and I cooked food and conducted a "food drive" for the community to raise money. People bought food and were very generous with donations. My family members contributed, and I returned to Angell Memorial with the money that I had raised. It wasn't enough for the surgeries, but the hospital agreed to perform the operations at a reduced rate.

I grew up with one cat, who ran away when I was ten years old. Bringing this cat that I've named Snow into my home has made me realize how much I was missing my former cat. I believe that Snow is very thankful for me being outside that evening and taking her in. Snow is a Javanese, which is a breed that is elegantly refined, sometimes fragile in appearance, but has a hard and muscular body with surprising strength. Snow's slender lines and flowing coat hide a rock hard body. Her coat never mats and rarely sheds. An occasional combing and bath to refresh the sensuous silky texture of her coat is all that is necessary outside of regular nail clipping. She is highly intelligent and is easy to care for.

Snow is now little more than a year old and has recovered nicely from her injuries. When I rescued her, she was skinnier than any cat I had ever seen. I almost wanted to cry. She was scared to go up and down stairs, and she was afraid of people. I had to do everything I could to make her not scared of them anymore. Now Snow is living as happily as can be. I take her for walks almost three times a day for an hour or two. She even sleeps with me because she knows no one is going to ever hurt her again. Snow is the best thing that happened to me, and I think I am the best thing that happened to her. I treat her with nothing but respect, and she does the same to me. I take her to the vet every month just to be on the safe side. We play together and sleep together. Rescuing Snow was one of the best decisions I ever made.

My Shy Birdie

Vrania Coelho

A YEAR AGO, my sister told me that someone she knew had a parrot. The owner of this parrot did not have the slightest idea how to take care of it. He was skinny, was not being fed enough proteins, was very frightened, and had an injured wing. There were several calls placed to the police station from neighbors because the parrot was always screaming and yelling. The police told the owner that they were going to take the parrot because of all the complaints. The police officer who went to the owner's apartment also told the owner that the parrot cage looked too small and that he should not be placed in such a small area. Most of the time, the owner had the parrot on the back of a chair, in a very small apartment in a neighborhood where people's homes were very close to each other and sound traveled easily.

The police were called to the house a few more times. And again I heard about it. I felt really bad because I did not want to see the parrot end up in a shelter or somewhere worse. I asked my sister to ask the owner if he ever thought of giving the parrot up for adoption. The owner was furious; he did not understand why we would ask such a question. One afternoon I went over to the house to visit the parrot and meet the owners. He looked so unhealthy, his color was dull, he was so skinny and very scared. No one could even move in the slightest way because he would jump and scream like someone was going to hurt him. I had never had a parrot before, but I could tell right away that he was being mistreated. Once again I asked the owner if he would consider giving the parrot up for adoption. Before the owner could say anything, I let him know that he was welcome to visit my home whenever he would like to see the parrot. He still looked angry, and I did not know what to expect. A few minutes later he agreed, but only "because of the police always being called here." I was so excited; I told the owner that I would be by later in the day to pick him up.

When I got him, he was scared, he opened his beak to bite me, and he would not let me or anyone else touch him. I played with him for a little while and gave him what are now his favorites: peanuts and sunflower seeds. He began to understand that I was not an enemy. When I brought

Birdie

him home, I placed him in my finished garage, and all he did was look around nervously. He stopped screaming and yelling because he was now in a quiet, secluded area with lots of trees. He was no longer around people who were always screaming. He now had his own space of freedom. We fell in love with him instantly. His wings were clipped, so we are able to bring him outside so that he can enjoy the warmth and sunny days. My little niece named him Birdie. The veterinarian told my fiancée and me that he was going to be fine, and that his wing would heel without needing surgery. The vet recommended food and nutrients that we should feed him.

The next few months, he started getting used to the family, and we started getting used to him. He was not flinching as much. He started to whistle and sing and act like a happy parrot. One year later, he still gets a little scared of strangers, but around the usual people he is fine. We pet him, play with him, and laugh with him. He even stands on our pool gate when we are swimming, because he does not want to be inside while we are having fun. When I adopted him, he did not say much, but now he says hello in a few languages; when we give him treats, he asks if you want some (he loves sharing); and when the phone rings, he says hello, and every time someone is on the phone talking, he keeps mumbling like he wants to get on the phone and have a conversation. He now stays in my home office because it is very spacious, and he loves being around us when we're home. If I could save an animal again, I would, because Birdie is a cherished part of our family.

Cat in the Rain

Heidi Porter

WHILE PREPARING TO face a second hurricane approaching Naples, Florida a few years ago, I was helping to prepare a waterfront restaurant for Mother Nature's wrath. During the preparation, a rescue worker was attempting to capture the new residents that had made their home under the building: the "restaurant cats."

As time was running out and Hurricane Charley was fast approaching, the staff learned that the mom and two of the three babies believed to be living under the building had been trapped. They would be safe under the building, and in the frenzy of the fast-approaching hurricane, that knowledge gave people a sense of relief. There was one

Calpurnia

holdout, however, a baby whom the rescue team feared that, owing to her independence, would battle the hurricane alone and refuse to be part of the rescue.

I told the woman in charge of the rescue that if that baby made it through, I had to have her. Of course, my husband saw it differently: He had no desire for a new family member.

Three days later, Hurricane Charley had worked his devastation on our area but spared the restaurant and the independent kitten. The trap that had been set just hours before the hurricane hit provided shelter for this tiny, coal-black, very upset baby. She was so small, she sat in the palm of my hand.

The staff could not believe she had lived for three days, at just three weeks old, alone through one of the worst hurricanes to hit the region. I knew that I just had to have the baby that had that type of will and determination to survive. She made her way through examinations and medication, maintaining her will to live.

After several weeks of us acclimating this tiny black fur ball to our home, one room at a time, she made the decision that she would accept the responsibility of running the house. Since her will and determination to make it in life was so strong, we decided her name should be Calpurnia, after the woman who is described in *To Kill a Mockingbird* as being "as black as the night," who also exercised the will and determination to accept many responsibilities. It just seemed fitting!

Dora the Adorer

Kimberly Raymond

FIRST MET Dora, a lovely Australian Shepherd mix when I was living in South Florida. My neighbors adopted her from a pet adoption mobile in the local Walmart parking lot. I remembered having concern because the family that adopted Dora had just recently rented the home next door to me. The husband, who was an alcoholic, had stayed only one month before returning to Indiana and left his wife "Susan" with four kids ranging in age from two to nine.

They had a cousin Ann, who lived locally and freely shared the history of the family with me. The three older kids, always appearing disheveled and dirty, came to my home almost daily, looking for attention and often food, both of which were freely given. Now Dora accompanied them and joyfully played with my two rescue dogs, Angus and Frankie. All I knew of Dora's history was that she was abused, and whenever an adult male would walk in the room, she would immediately

pee. The kids got angry with Dora when she peed in my house, believing I would be upset. I began to work with the kids and explained to them that the reaction was one she could not control and was probably because of past abuse. We worked together with Dora to help her feel safe.

An eight-foot-high stockade fence surrounded Dora's yard, and she would cry and try to dig under the fence whenever she heard us in the yard. Dora was left outside every day, rain or shine. Susan was more than happy to allow me to bring Dora over to play with Angus and Frankie whenever I wanted, and she authorized me to come get her from their yard at anytime. It was during one of these "play dates" that I became aware of potential neglect. I had brought out some dog treats and was surprised at Dora's apparent aggressiveness in gobbling the treats. I brought out some dog food and was horrified when I watched her literally vacuum up the food. There was no chewing involved and I had never witnessed the behavior before. When I returned her to her yard—which she never wanted—I checked her food and water bowl; they were empty. I filled them both and mentioned to the eldest son "Eric" about the need to be sure Dora had water during the day because every day in South Florida was hot. He assured me he would, and over the next couple days I checked her water bowl. It was always empty.

I immediately began to seek advice from various people as to how to handle this situation. Based on my experience and knowledge of the family, I felt that if I reported them to the authorities, they would know that I made the call since I was the only one who had access to the stockade "cell" Dora was kept in. Then they would most likely view me as a threat and cut off all contact with me, which in the long run would only hurt all of us, especially Dora. With the help of others, I decided to approach Susan, framing the issue as one in which I was sure that she, being so busy and Dora being Eric's responsibility, was probably not aware of, and asked her permission to work with Eric on how to properly care for Dora. I did feel guilty about this manipulation but did not know what else to do. Susan readily agreed with the plan and claimed to be completely unaware of the situation, laying all blame on her nine-year-old son. I tried to minimize the "fault" of Eric to Susan, rationalizing how kids sometimes just don't realize things. I apologized to Eric later when he was sent over by Susan to discuss the issue of Dora's care with me. I hoped I did not get him into trouble, but I did not know what else to do. Eric and I began to work together, and I purchased toys, a feeder, and one-gallon water dispenser to assist him. It appeared the water and food issue was resolved, and now I struggled only with Dora's seemingly unending struggle with loneliness, which I knew was really my issue. I knew that I had to accept the way some people interact with their family members and pets, even if I thought it was not the "right or best way."

Play dates continued as did frequent visits from the children, and then I learned the family was being evicted. Susan came by one evening to tell me the news and to let me know they would be moving into a motel for two weeks until they found another place. Although I had always treated Susan with respect and even helped them move, it was clear she was always on guard. Her plan for Dora was to have her stay with a *male* friend who lived in a small apartment, which did not allow animals. In addition, he was not home a minimum of ten hours a day.

During this visit, an adult male walked in the room and Dora, not yet over her fear, peed on the carpet. The smell was atrocious, and I told Susan that Dora might have an infection and would need to see a veterinarian. She replied that she had noticed that but did not have the money to take her in. I then offered to allow Dora to stay with us while they found a home and told Susan I would take Dora to the vet. Susan agreed.

The timing was not great, because I was going away, and Dora's fear of strangers—particularly men—meant that she would not do well with the people who were coming in to check on Angus and Frank. So I took her to a veterinarian office which also boarded dogs and explained the situation to them. On my return, they informed me she did have a severe bladder infection that they had been treating, and they told me they

Dora and her "new" brother Frankie

hoped I would get to keep her because she was such a wonderful dog. I was surprised at their comments because, although I loved Dora, the thought of three dogs seemed to be more than I could handle.

Two weeks turned into more than three months, and then came the day I had begun to dread. Although the family had only contacted me once regarding Dora, Susan showed up one day and told me they had found a home and wanted Dora back.

The home was two blocks from my house, and they would be moving in the next week. I did not want to let Dora go and asked if I could keep her, allowing the kids to come over anytime. She told me "no." The idea of three dogs no longer seemed a problem—we had slipped into a comfortable lifestyle and Frankie and Dora, very close in age, acted like a brother and sister who had known each other for a lifetime. I felt bad for judging the family in my mind, knowing, based on the information Ann had told me, plus my own experience with the family, that the cycle of neglect would quickly return. I hated having to deal with the entire situation. It would so much easier—I told myself—to turn a blind eye, give her back, and pretend none of it ever happened, but I knew I couldn't. I sought advice from a couple of local vets, who told me I had no right to Dora, and that by law I would have to give her back.

Resigned to this fact, I brought Dora to their new home. I tried to cheer myself that at least a chain link fenced enclosed the yard and maybe this new start would be different for the family, despite what Ann had told me. I cried on the way home because Dora frantically was trying to get in my car as I tried to leave. I went by a few times bringing Frontline™ and Heartgard™ medicine, a dog bed, and toys. Dora would always frantically try to get in my car the instant I arrived, and she would have to be locked in the fence or house in order for me to leave. It was incredibly painful for me, and I decided one last time to ask Susan if I could keep Dora because we missed her so much. Susan blankly said, "No, I'm sick of people like you thinking I can't take care of a dog." I felt bad for all of us and told her that was not how I felt, but I would not be coming by anymore because it was too painful for me.

Months went by, and I saw Dora only once. She was incredibly overweight at that time, and she was pulling Eric on his roller blades. I thought, *Well at least she is being fed and maybe he will be consistent with the exercise.* Then one night while sitting down to dinner, there was a knock on my door. The woman looked familiar, but I couldn't quite place her. "Kimberly, right?" she asked. "I'm Ann, Susan's cousin." I still could not place her until she asked, "Are you still interested in Dora?" She told me the dog officer had come and placed a notice on the door that day that they would be taking the dogs the next day. Evidently, Susan had reunited with her estranged parents who lived on the west coast of Florida and for the last two months had been leaving her now two dogs locked outside for extended periods of time without food and water. The neighbors had reported her on several occasions, but it appeared Susan did not care, being concerned only with reuniting with her parents whom I was told were affluent.

Ann told me she feared Dora would be put down if taken to the pound, and she thought I might still want her. To this day I do not know if that was true or if the concern was that Susan would have charges against her for neglect and in order to avoid that they sought my assistance. Ann told me she had keys to the house and the dogs were in the yard now without food or water. I grabbed some dog food and went over with her.

We could barely get through the fence because the dogs were hysterical. Dora would not stop jumping up on me. Having had a tenant who had abandoned animals in an apartment once before, I knew enough to throw the dog food across the ground so they would not attack each other. They both instantly inhaled the food and began to fight over the last bits. We broke that up and went into the house to get some water for the dogs and, as was the case with the last house I helped them move out of, this house was trashed but even worse. The air was stale inside, reeking of urine and garbage. There was trash everywhere and big flies buzzing around. There were cats inside without food or water, and I asked Ann to open the cans of cat food and feed and water them, which—looking back—I never thought about why she had keys but had not done so earlier.

Watching the dogs greedily drink water, I noticed these huge holes that had been dug under the cement slab of the home. Ann told me the dogs had done that, because, unlike the last home, this yard offered no

shelter from the beating sun or rain. She told me how one of the neighbors told her they had discovered the smaller dog had gotten his collar caught underneath the foundation and they had to crawl under to free him and did not know how long he had been trapped that way. The neighbors also told her how the dogs typically had to survive on a diet of their own feces, despite the attempts by some to provide some food or water between return visits of Susan. I didn't know what to do. I could not just take Dora and leave the other dog and cats.

Upon seeing the second dog, I immediately realized she looked just like a small version of Hogan, my neighbor Joan's dog. Joan often dropped by with Hogan for a visit. I remembered thinking, *I bet Joan would at least let this little dog stay with them overnight until we can figure something out.*

Some other friends showed up to help transport the dogs, but we realized we did not have leashes. I opened the back door of my little utility truck, and we tried to hold onto the dogs, but they bolted as soon as the gate was open. Despite all the time that had passed, Dora made a beeline for the back of my car. She jumped in, turned around, and as I approached to close the door, she looked at me as if to say, "What took you so long?" The little dog was quickly rounded up, and while Joan was being summoned, I began to give the small dog a bath.

Both dogs were filthy and coated with mud, and as I reached underneath to wash her belly, I felt stitches, which, based on Ann's story of when Susan got this dog, should have been long since removed. Joan arrived, and I am happy to report that she and her family instantly fell in love with this little dog that was clearly of the same breed as Hogan. Joan and her husband, both surgical nurses, removed the stitches and decided to keep her and name her Lucy. As for the cats, the animal control officer took them.

I bathed Dora and later that night sat on my bedroom floor snuggling her in my lap. She never took her eyes off mine, and as she gazed up at me, I promised her I would never let anyone ever hurt her again.

That was more than five years ago, and the three dogs and I have since relocated to New England. Although protective of our home, Dora no longer fears men, and to the surprise of our neighbors who saw her in the beginning, Dora has blossomed into a joyful and loving dog who can often be seen playing joyfully with toys by herself in the yard—an activity she had never engaged in before.

Five if by Land, Three if by Sea

Lindsey Sundberg

Pᴇᴛs, ᴀɴᴅ sᴘᴇᴄɪꜰɪᴄᴀʟʟʏ dogs, have, for as long as I can remember, been an integral component of my family. In fact, I would argue that one cannot define my family without including our dogs. This genuine connection to, and deep appreciation for, our dogs was instilled in my siblings and me at a very early age by my parents. Among the many important principles that my parents imparted to us were the value of caring for animals and the uniqueness of the reciprocal relationship that is at the heart of being a dog owner.

Dogs as family pets have been the one constant in my family. However, the act of adopting or rescuing dogs, which this book explores, did not take root in my family until the early 1990s. It was during that time that my mother became affiliated with a local Miniature Schnauzer (her favorite breed) Club in Atlanta, Georgia. The club served many functions, but it was its foster home program for abandoned and neglected dogs that opened our hearts and minds to the notion of "rescuing."

Although our family already had dogs that were obtained by traditional means (i.e. breeders), my mother was quite enthusiastic to open up our house to provide a much needed safe haven for Miniature Schnauzers who found their way to the reaches of the club. Essentially, my mother would accept one or two dogs at a time for a limited duration and ensure their safety, health, and comfort while permanent owners were located. It was a wonderful time in our household, especially for my brother, sisters, and me, as we always had the opportunity to enjoy the friendship of a new dog.

It was that early—and positive—experience through the Miniature Schnauzer Club that underscored the pervasiveness of the abandoned dog problem on the one hand and demonstrated to us the joy in "rescuing" dogs on the other. From that time on, "rescuing" dogs became more than a hobby for us; it became a natural extension of our collective love for dogs. More to the point, it became a *mission*.

As my family's experience highlights, there exists no single template for "rescuing" dogs. They enter your life at any given time, and when they do, there is often little opportunity for deliberation due to the seriousness of the dogs' conditions. You must either act or not, with the caveat being that if you decide on the latter course of action, it may have devastating repercussions for the particular dog. Please allow me to share with you some of those times that we did act!

Our "American" Dogs

Twixie

We adopted Twixie from a local PetSmart store that was hosting an "Adoption Day." Twixie was found on the highway in Dallas, Georgia, where it was presumed that she had been wandering for days. She was in rough physical condition. Among other physical deterioration, her hair was completely matted, and she was covered in ticks and fleas.

Twixie

The rescue group gave Twixie to us for free with the caveat that we had to have her spayed. Although there was some expense incurred because of the procedure, Twixie has been well worth it. In fact, as a practical matter, Twixie resembles a "lhasa-poo," a mixed breed that, because of its demand, is now quite expensive.

Some dog owners pay thousands of dollars for such a coveted mixed breed, but we were fortunate enough to obtain her without any financial considerations, save the spaying procedure.

Twixie is such a lovable dog, and she has immersed herself well in our household. With that said, she has her idiosyncrasies that point to her earlier abandonment. As an example, Twixie loves to hide her allotment of Greenies™ throughout the house. With the elapsing of a day or two, she frantically searches for the treats in her special hiding places. This action, in my estimation, is a reminder of a different life when her survival literally depended upon her success at securing food.

Madeline

Madeline (Maddie) is a Cairn Terrier mix. She closely resembles Toto from *The Wizard of Oz* except for her ears that flop down. Maddie was turned into the Cherokee County Animal Rescue Center when she was merely a couple of weeks old. Her owners decided that they did not want or could not keep their dog's puppies, hence Maddie's entrance into our lives.

Maddie was turned into the rescue center with her sister, who was adopted a day earlier. When my parents saved her, Maddie was no bigger than the palm of my hand. Although she continues to be the smallest dog of our pack, she exhibits alpha dog tendencies and is fiercely loyal.

Subsequent to any dog's spaying in our county, regulations require that a certificate verifying the procedure and accompanying check be filed with the town. After Maddie's procedure, my father forgot to file the necessary certificate and payment with our town. At some point relatively

Madeline

soon after the procedure, my father answered a call from the local sheriff's department during which he was threatened with jail time if they did not receive the necessary documents and check. Even though the misunderstanding was quickly resolved, you can imagine how thrilled my father was at the experience. I guess no good deed really does go unpunished.

Reese's

Reese's is thirteen years old, our oldest dog and the true matriarch of the family. For us, every day is her birthday because her fate was far from secured. Finding Reese's was a true chance encounter. My mother

Reese's

and sister were running errands, looking for a bird cage that was on sale at a pet store that was going out of business. My mother, always the curious shopper, peeked in and around the store and noticed a small Shih Tzu left in the kennel. She made an inquiry about the dog to the store employee who, in turn, informed her that at six p.m., the dog would be sent to the pound. My mother found this out at 5:55 p.m. She immediately decided to take the dog, much to my father's surprise when he returned home from work. However, my mom needed a birthday present for him, so guess what he got? A cute little puppy—a little different from the war documentary video he asked for.

Reese's quickly won my father over, as only she can do. In fact, they have a morning routine established. Reese's will accompany my father on his daily trips to Starbucks. My father will receive his coffee, and Reese's will receive her cookie from the drive-thru window.

Thirteen years later, Reese's continues to be sassy and emotional. It is hilarious to observe her after she is given a haircut. If she believes it is a bad one, she will face the wall and barely acknowledge us for a day or two afterward.

WeezyLou

I will preface this next story by declaring my unabashed love for WeezyLou. I love all my dogs, but I love Weezy just a little bit more.

She came to me from a Miniature Schnauzer rescue group, being the unfortunate product of a puppy mill in Oklahoma. Underestimating her severe medical condition and the subsequent medical bills, I saved Weezy as soon as I saw her dark black eyes and unusual white coat.

Weezy was only three pounds when I rescued her. At that point, she already had her tail and ears clipped. A puppy is not supposed to go under anesthesia until it is at a minimum five pounds. Surviving anesthesia at such an undeveloped age underscores Weezy's strength of spirit and resiliency, which still to this day characterize her. Two days after I brought her home, however, I observed that Weezy was battling a quickly worsening cough that just as quickly developed into a horrible wheezing (hence, her name), mucus-laden cough.

WeezyLou

Our veterinarian X-rayed her lungs and found that she had a serious case of bronchial pneumonia, with the prognosis looking bleak. The vet suggested I take Weezy to an emergency animal hospital to see if anything could be done to rid her of pneumonia. Well, after seven long nights in an incubator until her lungs regained strength while the antibiotics could cure the pneumonia, Weezy returned home. For the following three weeks after her hospital visit and $3,500 later, we had to inject shots of steroids in Weezy's back between the shoulder blades twice a day. I am proud to say that Weezy has completely recuperated; her weight is steady at fifteen pounds, and if appetite were a predictor of weight, she would be closer to fifty.

Weezy has so much to say! She is most excited when she sees her reflection in the mirror. One can deduce that she is very happy with what she sees. Well, that is my reasoning, anyway. If you were to ask my father, he would tell you emphatically that she is not the brightest dog in the pack and is barking because she believes her reflection is another dog.

Dixie

Dixie was not rescued or adopted in the truest sense of the words, but nevertheless, she has joined our household as a lovable, if somewhat misguided, Black Lab.

Before having children, my brother and his wife owned two Black Labs, Dixie and Dolly. When they had twins, two dogs became too much, and so, they were going to put Dixie, the more energetic of the two, up for adoption. Of course, my mother volunteered our house for Dixie.

Because of her size and athleticism, Dixie has the uncanny ability of getting into everything in the kitchen

Dixie

and allowing her appetite to take over from there. Among other items, she has enjoyed devouring our entire Thanksgiving turkey, bones and all, a half pound of raw salmon, and two sticks of butter.

An interesting by-product of Dixie's socialization into a dog pack of small terrier and Shih Tzu breeds is that she believes, wholeheartedly, that she is of similar size and weight. She loves to squeeze her sixty-pound frame into the other dogs' wicker beds as well as jumping into laps as though she were a ten-pound Shih Tzu.

Our "Sea" Dogs

Scupper

Three years ago, my parents purchased a condominium outside of San Juan, Puerto Rico. We believed the locale would provide us with a relaxing venue to vacation together. What we did not anticipate, however, was that word on the street traveled fast and far from Georgia to Puerto Rico: There was a family who loves dogs, any and all kinds, and provides comfy beds and great medical benefits.

Our first "sea" dog was literally waiting for my mom's arrival at the place. He came down the stairs wagging his tail and greeted her at the steps of the place, as though he were her dog already. He had no tags, was completely filthy, and was covered in fleas. We later found out from our vet in Puerto Rico that Scupper had heartworms, and it was not a good prognosis.

My mother brought him up to the roof, and it took her only one minute to decide what to do. She got away with keeping him because she let my dad name him. (That was a real bargaining tool.) Looking at him today and reflecting on what he was like when we first got him, the difference is like night and day. This dog lives the good life, has gained ten pounds, and has incredibly full and voluminous hair. When he first came to us, he would not touch a cookie or dog food, and he timidly stayed underneath the dining room table. He would not step foot in the bedrooms. Now, he'll bark silly until we give him a cookie after his walk in the morning, and he loves to be brushed!

Scupper

In order to bring Scupper back to Georgia, we had to buy an airline ticket for him for approximately seventy-five dollars. He could fly (as cargo only) only if it weren't too hot and there weren't already too many dogs on board. Before even being allowed to fly, he had to be examined by a veterinarian. We had to do this with each of our Sea dogs.

Zuleyka

Zuley was a true street puppy who was born eating iguanas and any type of trash she could find. My mom noticed her down by the beach one year after we took Scupper in. Since the beach was also near the security guard's booth, she assumed that the dog was his. Apparently not, for when mom asked in her rusty Spanish whose dog it was, he replied that she could take her if she wanted. So that was a no-brainer, and we named her after the 2006 Miss Universe

Zuleyka

winner, who was from Puerto Rico. Her ears stuck out all the time, meaning she was in a constant state of stress and always on guard. Now she rarely will have her right ear stick out—only in a serious situation. She is a tracker, which has caused us some stress, chasing after her when she sees a rabbit or bird. She looks just like a little Black Lab, and she gets along great with Dixie. The only time Zuley will howl is when Dixie barks. It is the sweetest thing.

Snickers

Snickers

My sister found Snickers two months later. She was someone's pet at one point in time, however, the condition she was in was not the kind of shape a pet should be in. She was completely covered in feces and matted all around, so much so that my mom had to completely shave her. She also had a brown tick disease that she could have potentially died from. Snickers resembles Madeline, and since Madeline absolutely adores my younger sister, following her *everywhere*, it was only fitting for her to take her to her home in D.C.

Conclusion

These anecdotes represent the true joys in our lives, and I cannot fathom what our days would be like without these dogs, but it would definitely be boring. I feel the dogs we have rescued have taught me more than I could ever teach them, such as unconditional love and the need to protect those that are innocent and vulnerable. For example, I no longer hold grudges against people. If a dog can snuggle with you at night and give you kisses just minutes after you discipline it, then I, too, can keep my tail "wagging" after my wrong-doings. And protecting those that need it extends beyond animals. It includes the shy person in class, the girl who tripped in front of a crowd, and the elderly woman who can't juggle her groceries and cane simultaneously. Observing and living with all kinds of dogs has improved my outlook on life, and I feel that I have become a more positive contributor to our society—a society that isn't as forgiving and accepting as my dogs are to me. Rescuing and rehabilitating dogs is not easy, but it is a very worthwhile and fulfilling task, and I recommend it to anyone.

3

You Have the Right to Remain Kind

MSLAW Students Performing On-the-Job Police Rescues

Honk, Honk, Goose

David Colby

AFTER A TYPICAL day shift in a suburban police department, I was traveling back to the station to write up the mound of paperwork that I had accumulated when dispatch called me advising me of some traffic tie-up on Lafayette Road. Grumbling to myself, with a few choice words under my breath, I took the call and headed to this particular section of Lafayette Road.

Lafayette Road is actually U.S. Route 1, which winds its way from Maine to Florida following the coastline. In many communities, it is a major thoroughfare lined with strip malls and gas stations, with lots and lots of traffic, most of which is traveling much too fast.

At my destination, I saw a woman pulled over to the side of the road with a look of hopelessness and fear on her face. I pulled in behind her parked station wagon and saw that her driver's door was still open, as she walked back and forth in front of her car. The woman saw me and ran full speed right at me. I started to think that this thirty-something woman was going to attack me. With all of the large trucks and cars rumbling by, I could not make out what she was saying as she approached. Just before I reached for my baton, I heard, "You have to help them." The woman was breathing hard and almost in tears on the verge of breaking down. I put my hands on her shoulders and asked, "Who needs my help?" fearing the response was that someone had been hit and was off in the ditch next to the road. "The geese!" she shouted into my face. Bewildered, I looked at her and asked, "Geese?" The woman—now crying—pointed to the area in front of her car. There I saw a mother goose and five goslings huddled together on the edge of the pavement. On our side of Lafayette Road was a patch of grass in front of one of the buildings; on the other side was a marshy area that the geese were trying to get to. The woman told me that the geese were eating on the grass and then tried to walk across the road. "I almost hit them, and no one will stop for me!" she said.

While I spoke to the woman, I watched as the mother goose attempted to walk her small charges across the road. Waiting for a break in the traffic, the mother goose started into the roadway. The five goslings were in a tight bunch behind their mother, their small fluffy bodies pitching back and forth as they waddled across the pavement. The goslings' awkward walk and downy fluffy bodies appeared in stark contrast to their mother's smooth brown feathers and strong powerful gait. Unfortunately, as the gaggle crossed the road, the children (as they so often do) started to dawdle behind their mother and would get stretched out across the roadway. The mother goose would turn around, open her wings, run back, and gather up her tiny ones as she went. Then a car would go charging by, leaving the whole small bunch shivering on the side of the road. Undaunted, the mother took a few minutes until the goslings stopped shivering and then started out for the road again. As she started, the woman next to me said, "I can't watch."

I got back into my cruiser and pulled it across the road in front of traffic and stopped all of the southbound traffic. This, of course, was met with a cacophony of horns and yells of "What the hell is going on?" And so the parade started. I got out of my cruiser and waved the traffic in the northbound lane to stop.

The driver of the first car that I had stopped in the southbound lane felt compelled to get out of his car and inquire (with a few terse comments) about the situation. I found myself responding to him with a few well placed quips of my own, and the driver readjusted himself back behind the wheel of his car, with his newly adjusted attitude for the situation.

Then we watched as the mother goose and her five fluffy little ones marched unmolested across the roadway, except for the one. One little gosling apparently liked the warm spring pavement on its little webbed feet and decided that the middle of the road was a good place to stop and enjoy the view, so it stopped and sat down in the center turn lane. The mother goose at this time was three quarters across the road and had not seen her gosling stop. With traffic backing up, I decided that this recalcitrant needed a little motivation to assist him across the road. Going back to my cruiser, I tapped the air horn, thinking that this would put some speed into the little one. The air horn gave out a loud blat. To my surprise, this did not scare the little one who had stopped. Not only did it not scare him or his brothers and sisters, but they also now looked at my cruiser as a great big black and white goose. All five of the goslings started to run towards my cruiser. The mother goose, now almost to the other side of the road, turned around and let out an ear-splitting honk of her own. All of the goslings in unison turned around and started back to her. Not able to believe what I just saw, and unable to contain myself, I just had to see if it would work again. I reached down and again tapped the air horn, and again the five little goslings turned around and started for my cruiser. This time, the mother was not amused one bit. Standing high on her feet with wings stretched and flapping, she again let loose with a loud "HONK!" The goslings responded immediately by changing their course and returning. Looking at the black-and-white menace, the mother bent her neck and hissed at the cruiser angrily.

Despite all of the traffic that was now backing up, I thought about hitting the air horn again, but good sense took over (and I didn't want to explain how my cruiser was damaged by an angry goose). Instead, I watched silently as the small contingent walked into the marshy area on the side of the road and out of my sight. I waved the traffic on and pulled my cruiser out of the road. Like a dam releasing rain water that has been held back too long, the flow of cars once again resumed its course and poured down Lafayette Road. With a beep and a tip of his coffee cup, the man in the car with comments roared past. In just a few seconds, the road was back to normal, and the small parade of geese was just as quickly forgotten. I walked over to the woman, who was now smiling. She said to me, "I did not know that you knew how to speak goose." I told her that until today, I did not know I could either. She got back into her car, and I could see in the back two small charges of her own. One was seated behind his mother in his car seat, with mushed up animal crackers in one hand and a half-full sippy cup in the other, cheering loudly for his mother. The other, tucked snugly into his car seat, head back, eyes closed and mouth open, slept through the whole event.

I held back the flow of traffic again just for a minute as the mother pulled out into traffic and too was gone. Now with the cars again rumbling along the road and the geese nowhere to be seen, I thought to myself, *Now that is something you don't see every day.*

Justice for One

Paul Watkins

Before attending the Massachusetts School of Law, I was employed as a municipal police officer. Fortunately, there were occasions when I believe I actually made a difference. Oftentimes law enforcement personnel fall into a false sense of belief that they are limited in their scope of employment, that they are "specialists." This is a very unfortunate yet common occurrence. A police officer may arrive at a scene, make an assessment, and say something like, "Well, this is a dog call; better call animal control," or "This is a case for D.S.S.," or my favorite: "Sir, this is a civil matter." Nothing could be further from the truth. The responsibility of a police officer is to protect everybody and everything within the jurisdiction. This is why cross-reporting and cooperation with outside agencies is so vital to successful law enforcement.

Once in a while everything comes together, and the story has a happy ending. Too often in law enforcement, however, there is no happy ending.

One early January morning several years ago, I was patrolling the city. I had recently applied for and obtained an arrest warrant for an individual who failed to register as a sexual offender. This guy had a criminal record dating back to the early 1970s and had been in and out of the state prison system for arson, fraud, sexual assaults, and robbery.

I saw a light on at the residence and attempted to serve the warrant. No one was home. I could definitely hear a faint scratching sound coming from within the apartment. Now I had a dilemma. What if he had a kidnapped woman inside? What if he were in need of medical aid? I did have an arrest warrant with the proper address, and I also had determined what I believed to be exigent circumstances. *Here we go again,* I thought. I obtained a key from maintenance and went in to a scene too horrific to describe.

The faint scratching was coming from a small mixed breed dog lying on the floor in a closed bathroom. The dog had obviously been neglected for some time. I drew my nightstick and searched the apartment for the man responsible. Fortunately for everybody's sake, I could not find him.

I also found a sickly parakeet and a fish tank with dead fish floating in it. There was no food or water available, and the stifling heat had transformed the apartment into a sauna. I knocked on some doors, and finally a neighbor assisted by providing some dog food and a water bowl.

By this time, the dispatcher was requesting my presence elsewhere, and I told him to hold all my calls. I contacted the Animal Rescue League via my cell phone, which was dispatching an ambulance! My sergeant arrived and began yelling and being abrasive, telling me I am not a dogcatcher, blah blah blah. I learned long ago that if you believe in what you are doing, and if it is the right thing to do, then do it and deal with the repercussions afterward. I explained the situation to my boss and told him I wasn't leaving until I was finished. He ended up leaving, muttering something about putting me on report. I didn't care. I ended up waiting about two hours, and the Animal Rescue League that responded was great. It took the dog and the parakeet for medical treatment.

I went back to the station, wrote a report, and the next day, I applied for a second arrest warrant for cruelty to animals. My fellow police officers did their usual verbal assault on work that they did not consider to be "police duties." At the time, the Massachusetts cruelty offense was only a misdemeanor, and it is very difficult to obtain an arrest warrant for anything other than a felony. But it actually turned out to be easy: I went to the court to a clerk magistrate who just so happened to be an animal lover. The warrant was issued forthwith.

A couple of months later, the Assistant District Attorney contacted me as he was convening a grand jury. I met with the neighbor and the guys from the Animal Rescue League, everybody testified, and we obtained an indictment for one count of cruelty to animals (the parakeet, unfortunately, was not covered by the statute.) The Animal Rescue League then said the dog needed a home. The neighbor volunteered to act as a temporary "foster parent."

In August, the defendant was convicted and sentenced to two years of probation. The neighbor was able to take full custody of the dog, and everything worked out for the best. I later learned from the woman at the Animal Rescue League that this was its first Superior Court conviction under the negligence prong of the cruelty-to-animals statute.

The defendant is presently incarcerated in a maximum-security prison for a subsequent conviction of indecent assault and battery. Because his probation for the cruelty-to-animals charge was violated, he was sentenced to one year in prison to run concurrent with his newest crime. So now this man is doing a year in state prison for what he did to (or failed to do for) that dog. That's justice!

Doe: Save Me

Robert Knapp

DURING THE EARLY hours of one cold December morning, I was dispatched to a rural part of the municipality to investigate a motor vehicle accident. The accident occurred in the Eastbound Lane of Marginal Road, a poorly lit and densely wooded part of town. While en route, I learned that the accident involved a vehicle that had collided with a deer. While this is not an uncommon occurrence, particularly on this stretch of roadway, I soon realized that this incident was far from the routine accident I was accustomed to handling.

The operator of the vehicle was uninjured; however, the deer was lying in the roadway, severely hurt but still alive. In my experience with handling accidents of this type, the injured deer possesses little, if any, chance of survival. However, the driver of the vehicle told me that the injured doe was pregnant and well into her gestational period. As a sworn officer with compassion for

wildlife, I could not consciously disregard this information and simply walk away.

Following unsuccessful efforts to acquire the services of a local veterinarian, I requested police dispatch to contact the Popcorn Park Zoo, a sanctuary for abandoned, injured, ill, and exploited wildlife. One of the zoo's primary objectives is to nurse wildlife back to health until such time as they may be released back into their natural habitat. Because the zoo is one of the few such sanctuaries in New Jersey, its services are in great demand, and I was unable to immediately procure its assistance.

Time was crucial. The extreme cold weather was surely compromising the survival of the mother. The death of the mother would give little hope for survival of her baby, depriving it of much needed nutrition and oxygen. The doe was unable to move and was lying in the middle of the roadway. In addition to my commitment to ensure the doe's safety, I had a responsibility to ensure the safety of motorists traveling on the roadway. With such poor lighting conditions, the injured doe presented a potential safety hazard to oncoming traffic. However, moving the deer might cause her to die, minimizing any chance of survival of the unborn fawn. Taking into account the time of the day and the volume of traffic that typically travels the road, I decided not to move the deer. As a precautionary measure, I erected a number of road flares in either direction to alert motorists of an approaching hazard.

While awaiting representatives from the zoo, I retrieved a blanket from my vehicle and covered the deer to keep her warm. Unfortunately, however, she succumbed to her injuries and died shortly thereafter. Zoo personnel were still some distance away and could not help at this juncture. The unborn fawn had approximately a fifty percent chance of survival, with that percentage declining the longer it remained inside the mother's uterus. It was essential that action be taken immediately if the baby deer had any chance of survival.

There was only one alternative left: perform a caesarean section on the doe. I returned to my patrol car to get blankets, gauze pads, an oxygen tank, a pediatric mask, medical scissors, tape, saline solution, and surgical gloves. First, I sterilized any metallic instrument to be used and which would potentially come in contact with the fawn. Next, I trimmed back as much fur as possible on the abdomen of the doe, rinsing the shaved area thoroughly with saline solution.

I made a four-to-five-inch horizontal incision just below the abdomen, followed by a second incision on the doe's uterus. Once I could see the baby deer, I slowly and carefully began to remove her. Upon successful extraction, I clamped the umbilical cord using a "flex-cuff" or what is commonly referred to as a "wire tie." Using sterilized medical scissors, I severed the cord just below the clamped area and wrapped the baby deer in a blanket.

Although the procedure had gone well, it was essential that I clear the fawn's nasal passages of any residual amniotic fluid. It is common in any form of birth that amniotic fluid obstructs the nasal passages of a newborn and if not removed immediately, it could eventually cause suffocation. Under medically controlled conditions, a "nasal aspirator" would normally be used to accomplish this; however, absent such equipment, I was required to improvise using what is known as an *Ambu Bag*.

An Ambu Bag is standard police issue equipment, used when performing Cardio Pulmonary Resuscitation (CPR). It consists of a large latex air chamber, or bag, attached to a mask and valve. When the bag is compressed, it forces air into the lungs and once the bag is released, it re-inflates and draws in ambient air. With a few on-scene modifications, I was able to allow the Ambu Bag to perform like a nasal aspirator. I inserted the tip into the fawn's nasal passage. The chamber was slowly released, causing a suction effect enough to draw out the amniotic fluid that would otherwise compromise the fawn's breathing. A pediatric oxygen mask was held several inches from the mouth and nose of the deer to further assist the fawn's breathing. Direct placement would cause the deer to be startled, and to avoid injury, it was essential to restrict the newborn's movement. Fifteen to twenty minutes later, representatives from the Popcorn Park Zoo arrived on scene and took custody of the young fawn. I learned later that the young fawn did in fact survive and is expected to develop into a full-grown healthy doe.

A Little White Lie and a Life of Love

Richard Howe

WHILE ON PATROL one night in the fall of 1993 in Brattleboro, Vermont, I received a call reporting that some stray cats had been struck by a car, which had left the scene. When I arrived, I found five kittens on the roadside; four of them appeared to be dead. The emergency on-call veterinarian confirmed that they were. The fifth kitten had scrapes and was a little banged up but didn't appear to have any serious injuries. The veterinarian told me that it looked as though the kittens were probably thrown from a moving car. All of them were very malnourished and had obviously been abused.

Samantha, sharing the author's cantaloupe

I then went to put the lone kitten in a cage for the night. But I just couldn't do it. I guess I'm a sucker because I took the kitten and asked my dispatcher to call my wife at home and tell her I was on the way with a kitten. When I arrived, my wife and I cleaned her up and fed her milk. She fell asleep right away. I told my wife that the veterinarian was looking for a home for her, and we would keep her temporarily. The truth is, I lied; no one was looking for a home. I had told the veterinarian that I would be her home. Errin had been homesick and missed the cat that she had grown up with, and I figured this couldn't hurt.

The kitten endeared herself to us right away. One day, I was eating cantaloupe and left half of it on a plate in the living room while I got up to do something. I came back, and the kitten had stuck her small head completely inside the remaining half of the cantaloupe, licking and eating what she could. (To this day, she loves it, along with yogurt and ice cream, which my kids love to feed her.)

It didn't take long for me to tell Errin that I had told a white lie. By then it was too late anyway: Samantha was part of our family and established her place as such. When I was assigned the police department's rescue tracking and narcotics dog two years later, Samantha wanted nothing to do with Red, who was very friendly. She would sit at the top of the stairs and stare at Red, whom we kept at the bottom of the stairs, behind a baby gate. Eventually, Samantha worked her way to the bottom of the stairs and would stand right behind the gate, just a few inches away from Red. Within a few weeks, they became inseparable.

Samantha has been with us for fifteen years now, and I'm proud that she's had a pretty good life considering how it started.

Officer, Take a Boa

John Katsirebas

IT WAS DUSK. I was ten hours into a twelve-hour shift and tired from a long day of what seemed like constant calls for service. I was tied up on a motor vehicle stop, so the call went to Officer Jones.

I heard the call as it came in over the radio. "I need a unit to respond to 23 Franklin Street for a reported ten-foot python terrorizing the neighborhood. The complainant advised she has the animal cornered beside her shed, holding it at bay with a rake." There was a short pause then Officer Jones radioed back that he would be en route and expected to arrive on scene within five minutes.

Officer Jones is a large and intimidating man. He's a tough cop and always gets the job done. I have seen

Snuggles

him in action on countless past occasions, and his courage in the line of duty is unwavering. But it's no secret that Officer Jones hates snakes. In fact, he has been known to take the longer way around when a grass snake has been sighted in the immediate area. A rubber toy snake, if placed in the right desk drawer, is a guaranteed laugh if you are amused by seeing a grown man scream like a child.

I released my detainee and called Officer Jones on the radio, asking if he would like some assistance. Officer Jones answered, "I'm all set. It's nothin' a little buckshot can't handle." I turned my cruiser around and headed for Franklin Street, hoping I would get there in time or maybe even before Officer Jones.

I rolled up onto the scene to find Officer Jones standing by the shed pointing his shotgun at the ground in front of him. The gun was shaking slightly, and I could not help but wonder why he was hesitating. I would later discover that he was so nervous that he had forgotten to disengage the safety and was squeezing the trigger angrily, hence the shaking. I called his name suddenly and loudly, causing him to jump a bit and let loose with a colorful expletive. He composed himself, turned to me, and demanded, "WHAT?!"

I carefully placed my hand on Jones' shotgun and asked, "Mind if I try to deal with this suspect? Without gunfire?" Officer Jones answered, "Whatever, man. Just don't get mad when I laugh when you get bitten." I looked down at the terrified snake. It was a very pretty red-tailed boa constrictor and was only about four feet long. It was very upset and was striking blindly at any person or object that came into range. I asked the homeowner if I might borrow a pillow case, and she happily obliged.

With a flashlight and the pillowcase in my left hand, I waved the items to get the snake's attention. When I was reasonably certain that its attention was fixed on my left hand, I grabbed the snake under its jaws with my right. In the same motion, I slid the snake into the pillowcase and let go.

The homeowner was delighted that the police did not open fire in her backyard. Officer Jones was equally delighted as he was under the impression that we would now take the pillowcase to a nearby sand pit where he could blast the snake while it writhed helplessly in the bag. He was very disappointed when I told him I would take the snake home with me and care for it until its owner could be identified.

The owner never came forward. Snuggles is now almost eight feet long and lives a happy life. I have had her for five years now, and she has not struck at a human being in anger or fear since the night she was rescued.

4

The Fat Lady Hasn't Sung

Stories that don't quite fit, but are too good to omit

Cane Made Us Able

Paul Franzese

I KNOW THIS BOOK is supposed to be about how I saved an animal, but the truth is I have never done so. However, an animal has indeed saved my family and me. My Yorkshire Terrier-mix named Cane didn't save us from a burning home or a thief in the night trying to get into the house; it was our minds and hearts that he saved during a time of loss and mourning.

Cane

My family, especially my father, had always wanted a dog for as long as I could remember. The one person who wouldn't stand for it was my mother. This isn't because she hated animals or didn't want some little fur ball being her new companion; it was simply because I grew up in the most immaculate, well-kept house since birth, and my mother was not about to take the chance on having a dog soil our home. My dad was the one who truly wanted a dog and never got one solely out of consideration for my mother. Later he would try to persuade her by showing her cute dogs and promising he would take sole responsibility for the dog's needs; she was soon about to give in.

Tragically, however, on January 9, 2006, my mother passed away. She had a heart attack while she was sleeping. It was totally unexpected. Even though my entire extended family is one huge support system, and our way of dealing with sadness is by making each other laugh, there was a certain kind of unspoken sadness that filled the air of our cherished home. Everyone in our family would come over and spend time with us, but once everyone left, there was something missing in the home for my father, sister, and me.

I was graduating college that year at Sacred Heart University and had to return to Connecticut to finish my senior year. I suppose my father and sister felt a certain kind of loneliness when I was gone because they were both out of the house so much, almost as if there was nothing to go home for. About three months after my mother's death, my father said, "You know what? I'm getting a dog." Then along came Cane, a Yorkie-mix puppy.

My little cousin Alessandra would always pick out dogs and identify them as "cane" ("kah-nay"). The word *cane* means dog in Italian, so technically speaking, my dog's name is actually Dog. Whenever Alessandra would say that, even when my mother was still here, my dad would say that if we ever got a dog, his name would be Cane. So really, she is the reason for his name.

It's not as if we got our dog as a replacement for my mother, but when she passed, we had lost something huge. My mother was fun and playful and had a huge impact on our lives. When we lost her, we all lost a part of ourselves. My dad explained that he just wanted to have a sense of home again, and that to him was home cooking and a dog running around.

Nobody in my family will ever get over the devastation of what happened, but there are ways to turn a negative into a positive. Cane was that little beam of light for my family during a dark time. His playfulness and love now give a reason for my family and me to come home and be together. He doesn't know it, but not only did he save one person, he also saved an entire family.

Ay, Chihuahua!

Denise Eddy

GROWING UP I had a fear of animals. I was frightened of dogs, cats, and even fish. I believe it was because at a young age, I developed a very high fever and, while I was hallucinating, I saw different animals and fish in my bed. I remember asking my grandmother to remove the fish from the bed. I have never been able to erase those images, so each time my son requested a pet, my response was never in the affirmative.

The summer prior to Christopher's first year in college, he woke me with the news. "I now have man's best friend!" I was sleeping; his announcement was of no delight. Christopher realized the mistake immediately; with the twelve-hour time difference, it was 2:30 in the morning.

Nevertheless, the dialogue began. "Remember growing up, you never let me have man's best friend? Well, I bought a dog!" My reaction was one of shock, dismay, and anger. I asked what he proposed doing with this dog in the fall. "You're going away to school. You can't leave a dog home with me. I travel for business. Who's going to take care of this dog? I can't. I suppose you think I'm going to hire someone to take care of this animal?" When the conversation was over, I was not happy. But then he knew I would not be pleased. Each time Christopher tried this, the animal went back.

During each call from overseas, Christopher's sales campaign continued. *The dog was "small," two pounds, just a puppy. He will never get bigger than three or four pounds. The dog is healthy. I went to a professional breeder to buy the dog. You will love Cheech.* Now, the dog had a name: Cheech. After all, it's a Mexican dog. Christopher seemed different this time; I could not reason with him. Even the college argument had little effect. "Do you think this dog is going to college with you?" The answer was a resounding "Yes!"

Each day Christopher continued to tell me how happy he was. He never failed to remind me that I never allowed him to have "man's best friend." My guilt was overwhelming. I was always traveling for business, and he was alone with no dog for companionship.

Upon my return to the States, I met Cheech. He was really cute but high strung. Christopher has never admitted how much he paid for Cheech. In fact, he had to have an interview with the breeder before he was allowed to buy the dog. He also needed an adult to attest to his character and responsibility. I soon realized this dog was staying. There was nothing I could do.

The summer was going by fast. Christopher was due to leave for school in August, and of course no dogs were allowed in the dorm. So the hunt began to find an apartment that would allow a dog. We searched and searched. Either there was no availability or no dogs allowed. Finally, a townhouse became available. I got the call and was on a plane the next morning. I had asked property management to fax a copy of the lease. On the plane, I read that cats were allowed but not dogs. I was determined as school was fast approaching. Somehow, I was going to convince this man to allow Cheech. This was to be the biggest sales job of my life.

I went right to the apartment complex when I landed. The manager showed me the apartment. He was quite impressed; I had flown there only to see the apartment. He had no idea how panicked I was. He asked if I was ready to sign the lease. "Are you taking it?" he asked. He was shocked when I told him there was one problem with the lease: "Christopher has a dog, and he is not going anywhere without it." I explained that I traveled for business, and he could not leave the dog at home. Besides, he was not parting with "man's best friend." Finally, I convinced the manager to write into the lease, "one cat-sized dog" allowed. In August the boys, Christopher and Cheech, were off to college.

I must admit, I became very attached to Cheech. I fell in love with this dog. I looked forward to the boys coming home for vacation. In fact, I was the one to bathe the dog as soon they arrived home. Although he was really Christopher's dog, I loved him. No one was more surprised than I that I grew attached to that little dog.

Cheech was only four years old in the summer of 2005. I was in Arizona on business when Christopher called. He thought Cheech was not feeling well. The dog wasn't eating and just did not seem right. Since they spent so much of the year there, the dog had a veterinarian at school. I told Chris to take Cheech to the vet, but I never imagined what was to come. The vet said he was unsure of what was wrong with the dog, but he was sure he needed fluid. He would need to keep Cheech overnight. Of course, I agreed.

The next morning Chris called. Cheech had had a seizure. The vet was unsure but thought he had either a brain tumor or meningitis. He wanted to do an MRI and a spinal tap. The cost of the MRI was $2,600. I suggested trying the spinal tap first to rule out the infection. The vet didn't want to do that because the dog was just so small, he was afraid of puncturing an organ. I asked if he could treat this clinically with antibiotics for 24 hours. The vet felt it would not change the outcome, unless it was an infection, at which point I asked, "This dog isn't going to die, is he?" The answer was one I was not prepared for: "Fifty/fifty." It was shock and disbelief.

Cheech

Certainly, I really never expected to hear that. I never thought the dog would die. The dog was still a puppy in my mind.

Christopher was going to visit Cheech two hours later. He was just about to leave when the call came. Cheech was dead. Not more than two hours after our phone conversation, the dog was dead. I think I was in disbelief more than shock. That night I boarded the first flight back to the east coast. I flew all night and landed at 10:30 the next morning.

Certainly, as I flew cross-county, I was distraught at losing the dog. But more ominous was the knowledge of just how devastated Christopher would be. He was more inconsolable than I had feared. Cheech had been with him from the time he left for college. He was physically and emotionally sick. He hadn't slept since the night Cheech died.

Two days later, Chris was still not ready to make a decision regarding Cheech's remains. He didn't want to cremate Cheech ("I don't want to burn my dog"), and the pet cemetery would only pick up pets that died in the state. I wasn't about to drive the body back to

Massachusetts, so that option was out. I needed to fly back to Arizona.

Finally on Sunday morning, I picked Christopher up at his apartment. He got into the car with Cheech's favorite toy, a small stuffed lamb. Then I knew that he had decided. He agreed to cremation.

The staff at the hospital was wonderful. They put us in a small room and explained that Cheech would be stiff and cold. They brought Cheech to us. He was lying on a tray with a plaid wool blanket around him. Chris and I both cried. Christopher placed the lamb with Cheech, kissed him goodbye, and left the room. I couldn't stop crying. Finally, I kissed Cheech and left.

It was so hard to see Christopher this devastated. Cheech was not only his dog but his roommate, best friend, and companion throughout college. The loss of Cheech was far more devastating than I could have ever imagined.

I never wanted an animal, yet I was an emotional wreck at the loss of Cheech. This was the animal I fought so hard not to have. I tried to tell myself that I never wanted this dog. No logic made any difference. The loss was tremendous. It was as though a family member had died. In fact, that is what happened. I had fought and resisted a dog for years, finding every reason imaginable why it was a terrible idea. I allowed my travel schedule, my fear of animals, and the mere inconvenience of a dog dictate. I was adamantly opposed to the very idea of an animal. Ultimately, Cheech won my heart, and now I wish for another Cheech.

Fluffy, the Mom Saver

Jo-Ann Andaloro

"If animals could speak the dog would be a blundering outspoken fellow; but the cat would have the rare grace of never saying a word too much." —MARK TWAIN

RARE GRACE, NOT this cat! He was a puff of fur on his birth, barely able to hold his head up for the weight of his coat. His first steps were far from graceful, as he fell forward on his head most days, always a little behind the rest of the litter. Resembling an inverse skunk, he was snow white with a proud black stripe bisecting his stout frame. Running, pouncing, and jumping were not his strong points. Yet, at meal time, he excelled in his pursuit of the food bowl, clamoring over his siblings to be first in line. He grew strong and chubby, earning his creative yet distinctive name of Fluffy the Cat.

Who knew that this meager beginning would produce a future hero. After all, Fluffy spent most days basking in the sun, looking for his next rubdown and his next meal. He followed us everywhere, even if it meant getting up from the couch. He was as independent as he was dependent, and he was my mother's companion in her elder years. When she got home at night, Fluffy was there. He would meow and purr unconditionally. When she brought groceries home, he would climb into every bag to pull out the day's plunder. When she watered plants, he would jump and roll into the planter until his fur was saturated in mud.

As my mother aged and her memories faded, Fluffy was there. When she went outside, he would escort her about the yard. He would keep a watchful eye, marking the perimeter with his big downy paws, never allowing her to wander too far from him. He was always there, inclusive of the day he became her hero.

It was a day like any other, nothing special in the air. Mom and Fluffy headed outside to water a few plants, unsuspecting of what would happen next. When she turned her back, a dog of great size, strength, and anger had emerged from nowhere, lunging toward her frail and elderly body. As she was about to be trampled, a squealing war cry emerged from the ground before her. It was Fluffy, up on her hind legs, mouth and claws open with the vigor of a mountain lion, leaping across the dog's path and onto his head like a muzzle. Fluffy attached himself to the dog's being and would not let go until the dog fled the yard and his companion was safe.

Fluffy

Neighbors witnessing the commotion and this great feat of will and resolve could not believe this mild-mannered fur ball rose to the rank of protector and defender. David defeated Goliath again that day, and he saved my mom in the process.

Fluffy did not return home for two nights despite our diligent search, and we feared the worst. Days later, we found him under some overgrown shrubs: panting, disoriented, and unable to lift his head for the weight of his swollen body. The ordeal had sent him into congestive heart failure (CHF), and his enlarged heart was unable to pump efficiently. In humans, once past an acute crisis, CHF is manageable with medication, lifestyle changes, and exercise. However, exercise and Fluffy were not words commonly heard in the same breath. How do you get a cat to make lifestyle changes? Pavlov would surely have an easier time proving his hypotheses than getting Fluffy onto a treadmill.

Fluffy never became that long distance runner we had hoped for, but with good medical care, a loving home, and a devoted companion, this hero lived many happy years. When it was his time to pass on, a grateful family who appreciated his unselfishness surrounded him. In his bravery, he left a legacy: Get involved, help one another, live your life, and never miss a meal. More important, he inspired our family to assist the local shelter in providing foster care to abandoned kittens. Despite loving each one of them and the sadness of separating upon their adoption, we hope this small act in honor of such a brave cat will make a difference.

A Peck of a Bird

Kurt Olson

GREGORY PECK WAS a great actor; he was also my first bird. Coincidentally, the actor had an association with birds in that his greatest role was in *To Kill a Mockingbird* as Atticus Finch, the noble father figure who did his best to instill a sense of morality and justice in those around him. Gregory Peck—the actor—always did the right thing.

The less well known Gregory Peck was a baby-blue-fronted Amazon parrot. A bird bred for the jungle and rescued from those dangers only to be exposed to the hazards of urban living. While this story is not as important as are the lessons provided by Atticus Finch, it is worth recognizing that there are dramatic consequences when we rip native-born species from their natural habitats in Brazil's rainforests to indulge our desire to hear "Polly wants a cracker."

Gregory Peck was just a baby when my then girlfriend, Rola, and I got him. In some small way he satisfied her maternal instincts. While in different circumstances she may have preferred a puppy or a baby-white-fronted human, those were not viable options, as we had neither the time nor patience then for those life-changing complications. I fell to her pleas to get him. I figured a bird could not possibly be that difficult anyway. Gregory Peck soon proved me wrong, however, by injecting some sobering time management issues into our lives.

Rule number one about caring for a bird: They poop a lot. If bird poop were a natural resource, we would have been knee deep in money. Gregory Peck pooped and pooped until the tray at the bottom of his cage would fill again and again with the stuff. It was an odorous and caustic chore.

Rule number two about caring for a bird: Bird poop is poisonous for humans. It may not be poisonous for birds, but who wants to see Gregory Peck strutting around in his poop, picking out the leftover fruit scraps that fell into the bottom of the tray. So wear gloves, hold your nose, and bring a big barrel when it is time to clean the cage. I have come to learn that while there are certain hazards, it is far easier to change the occasional diaper than to keep a bird's cage clean.

Rule number three about caring for a bird: They make a lot of noise. Like roosters who crack the dawn's early light with their cock-a-doodle-doos, Gregory Peck would start his hysterical screeching at first light. Though birders like to refer to the sounds made by their feathered friends as "songs" or "calls," Gregory Peck's sounds were not akin to the velvety sounds made by Nora Jones or Frank Sinatra. They were more like the bloodcurdling sounds of your neighbor being strangled to death. We were told that if we kept his cage dark with blankets, he would be fooled into thinking it was still nighttime and would stay quiet. Gregory Peck, however, was no fool. When the clock struck five a.m., he knew it was time to start "singing." When we moved, our neighbors bid us a tearful goodbye, but some say they were tears of joy.

Gregory Peck's penchant for vocalizing did, however, lead to some genuinely fabulous or forgettable moments depending upon your perspective. He would say things like "Hey, your pants are on fire," "Give me a peanut, or I'll slap your face," and "When you touch me, oh baby, you know what I like!" One time the mailman came to our door and rang the bell. When no one answered the bell quickly, the mailman opened the slot on the front door and slid the mail through the slot. When he did, Gregory Peck began his litany of colorful phrases. The mailman slowly walked away shaking his head and muttering that "some people just don't know how to behave."

Rola enjoyed hanging around the house in her birthday suit when she did household chores. Even in New England during winter, she would simply turn up the heat to clean the house. Rola would release Gregory from his cage and let him fly around the cathedral ceiling while she ironed, vacuumed, washed, dried, and dusted. Maybe it brought out her primal feelings—hooking up with Tarzan and careening around on long vines through moss-covered trees to the screeches of the jungle birds. She would clean, Gregory Peck would screech, and life was good.

Suddenly, a knock on the door announced a visitor. "Package delivery, ma'am," the husky voice at the door said. "Just a minute," Rola replied as she covered herself in a towel and slowly opened the door. At just that second, Gregory Peck flew right out the front door into the hustle and bustle of a New England winter, not exactly a hospitable place for a baby-blue-fronted parrot. Resplendent in his Amazonian colors and descended from prehistoric ancestors, Gregory Peck flew fast to freedom. Despite the chill in the air, he continued on—only 4,000 more miles, and Gregory Peck would be home at last.

My phone at work rang, "Gregory Peck just flew out the front door. Get home fast," Rola said in between her tears and gulps of breath. "He's going to die. You've got to find him." And with that I knew that Gregory Peck was gone.

Saddened by my loss, but in an odd way excited at the thought of Gregory Peck's newfound freedom, I stood paralyzed in inaction. Just then, my neighbor Dan came into my store and said, "The police radio just said a blue parrot is buzzing the people in line at the movie theatre on Main Street—any idea where your stupid bird is?" I locked the door, raced down the street and began to look around frantically. Finally, just a few feet from the theatre ticket window, shivering and looking a trifle discombobulated, was the most beautiful parrot I had ever seen. As I picked him up and cradled him in my arms, I looked up to see what was playing: *The Birdman of Alcatraz.*

A Diamond Is Forever

Bronwyn Ford

THERE'S PROBABLY SOME truth in the statement that all of philosophy can be reduced to the single question of whether to live or die. It's a choice most of us, most of the time, hardly seem conscious we're making from moment to moment, perhaps because the answer is just too easy, or because we're simply too busy doing other things. Once I made that choice for someone else. I learned that, to the extent that we become what we love, the result I made was the same choice for part of myself. I still haven't decided if the choice strengthened or diminished me. Even when an event is inevitable, and we feel prepared for the expected because we've grasped on some intellectual level that things will be different afterwards, the truth is, there's no way of knowing what it's like for someone to be gone until he's gone, there's no good time to say goodbye to someone you love, and after it actually happens, when the hope associated with the uncertainty of not knowing is gone, there's no avoiding the agony that remains upon realizing that things will never be the same. Many times since, maybe seeking solace in platitudes, I've remembered a summer before I made the choice, when a girl at a barn where I was working told me about a poster she had of a beautiful horse and a quote that said, "In the end, everything is okay; if it's not okay, it's not the end." Believing things will be okay, no matter how unbearable they may seem, is faith. In the meantime, waiting for things to be okay is a kind of purgatory: What is done is done, and judgment is suspended for the time being.

I kept my horse named Goldie at a barn where there was a black pony named Diamond. Diamond belonged to a young girl and became slightly lame. His owners didn't want to spend any more money trying to diagnose his problem, so the veterinarian said Diamond shouldn't be ridden but would be okay as a companion for another horse. They offered Diamond to me for free, but I gave them a few hundred dollars because I didn't want them to think he was worth nothing. He was old even then in equine terms, thought to be in his late thirties.

Five years later when spring came, Diamond didn't shed his winter coat. He got antibiotics for his congestion, which recurred as soon as the medicine was gone. He got different feed, more medicine, more tests. He became borderline diabetic, then stopped eating. When I called the vet, he said I had to make a decision that day. I told him I couldn't decide anything until I saw the pony. He agreed to meet me at the barn that afternoon.

I had never put an animal down. The vet didn't seem to understand my hesitation. I tried to explain I felt as if euthanizing the pony would be killing him, interfering with the process, rushing him through his last moments. I didn't understand what was cruel about

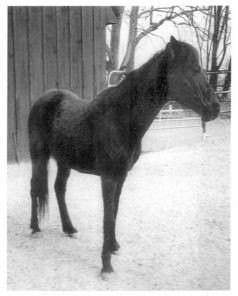

Diamond

letting nature take its course. The vet said the pony was suffering, that he'd live one more day at most. He said that if he left, he wouldn't come back. He said that if the pony went down in his stall he'd have to get the back hoe, that if I couldn't do this, then I shouldn't have horses. I figured the opposite: A person who finds it easy to kill an animal should never be allowed to have one.

My horse and pony lived on someone else's property, people who trusted the vet and respected his opinion. He waited for the hour and a half it took for me to make a decision. I wanted to do what was best for Diamond, not just hold on to him selfishly.

When it was over, the vet apologized for being hard on me and said I could blame him. I told him I didn't need to blame anybody: I made what seemed to be the right decision at the time, and I'd live with it.

The owners of the barn paid a man to take Diamond's body away and bury him. Someday I'll go there.

The barn owners cut some long black hair from Diamond's tail and gave it to me, along with his halter and a photo taken when he came to the barn. He arrived in April. He died in April. I was born in April. And my birthstone is a diamond. I think T. S. Eliot may have been right when, if my memory serves me well, in his poem "The Waste Land," he wrote: "April is the cruellest month, breeding / Lilacs out of the dead land, mixing / Memory and desire, stirring / Dull roots with spring rain."

Maybe things would have been different if Diamond had been on my own land. I don't understand what purpose it would serve to feel guilt, but I can't help but wonder how many breaths I deprived him of; how precious was his last one; how I can compare them to the number of mine I've wasted on harsh words and games and nonsense; whether he felt as if I betrayed his trust, and if so, if he knew how sorry I was about that; and when people ask about my pets and I rattle them off, what it is that still makes me often add, "I had a pony, too, but he died."

To love is to take the biggest possible risk, not because we may outlive its object, but because we never know how loving will change our lives. Refusing to love someone because he or she won't live forever isn't a valid alternative. Maybe Diamond wasn't made immortal because I loved him, but, in some way, he has become immortal now, because I love him still.

Professors Sullivan, Vietzke, and Coyne founded ARC to create a coalition of like-minded people to support animal rights activity.

The Massachusetts School of Law helped to establish ARC, whose headquarters are located at the Massachusetts School of Law.

The Massachusetts School of Law provides technical and administrative support consistent with its mission to have professors and students engage in community service and in related public interest projects.

ANIMAL RIGHTS COOPERATIVE is an organization committed to the humane treatment of animals. Our organization and its members are committed to working individually in personal ways and collectively through cooperative efforts to:

1. Ensure the humane treatment of all animals.
2. Save the lives of animals.
3. Push for passage of a declaration on animal welfare by the United Nations. This declaration would be patterned after the European Union's Amsterdam Protocol, which states that all animals are sentient creatures, meaning that they are living, and living things have feelings and in particular feel pain.

For more information, visit www.animalrightscoop.com.

The Shadow Fund

Shadow is a five-year-old yellow Labrador Retriever that Robert Burke rescued two years ago. Mr. Burke, a fifty-six-year-old Vietnam Veteran was going to be forced to quit his job so he could access his 401(k) retirement plan (his company does not permit current employees to access the account) to pay for surgery that Shadow needed, since he could not pay for it on his $488 weekly salary. Fortunately for Mr. Burke and Shadow, however, Mark E. Vogler of the *Lawrence Eagle-Tribune* wrote a story about Burke's predicament. The story attracted the attention of the Massachusetts School of Law and Dr. Richard Lindsay, founder of the Andover Animal Hospital. After examining Shadow, Dr. Lindsay agreed to perform the surgery if the law school could raise $1,000 to cover part of the cost. That was all Diane Sullivan needed to hear, and she and her animal law class spread the word. People sent in so much money that there was a surplus after paying for the surgery. Thus, The Shadow Fund was established at the suggestion of Associate Dean Michael L. Coyne and Burke to help pet owners who cannot afford necessary medical treatment for their pets.

The Shadow Fund
c/o Massachusetts School of Law
500 Federal Street
Andover MA 01810